D1097785

THE COWBOY ENCYCLOPEDIA

The
COWBOY
ENCYCLOPEDIA

The Old and the New West
from the Open Range to
the Dude Ranch

by

BRUCE GRANT

Illustrated by
JACKIE & FIORE MASTRI

Cover by CLARK BRONSON

Rand McNally & Company
New York CHICAGO San Francisco

LIBRARY OF CONGRESS CATALOG CARD NUMBER: 51-10382

ACKNOWLEDGMENTS

For the use of quotations in the text acknowledgment is made to the following:

APPLETON-CENTURY-CROFTS, INC. for permission to use a quotation in the article on "Bronco Buster" from *Story of the Cowboy*, by Emerson Hough. Copyright, 1897, by Appleton-Century-Crofts, Inc. • THE BOBBS MERRILL COMPANY, INC. for permission to use a quotation in the article on "Hickok" from *Story of the Outlaw*, by Emerson Hough. Copyright, 1907, by The Bobbs Merrill Company • THE CAXTON PRINTERS, LTD. for permission to use a quotation in the article "Pecos Justice" and a quotation in the article "Long Rider," both from *Triggernometry*, by Eugene Cunningham. Published by The Caxton Printers, Ltd., Caldwell, Idaho. Used by special permission of the copyright owners • JOE DE YONG for a quotation from a manuscript in the article "Eagle" • MR. J. FRANK DOBIE for a quotation in the article "Cattle King" • HAMLEY & COMPANY for permission to use pictures of western gear from their catalog • HARPER & BROTHERS for use of a quotation in the article "Pony Express" from *Roughing It*, by Mark Twain • MRS. RUBY TERRILL LOMAX for permission to use a quotation in the preliminary pages and to use quotations in the articles "Chuck," "Curlew," "Cowboy," "Dogie," "Hoecake," "Texas Rangers," and "Cowboy Songs," all from *Cowboy Songs and Other Frontier Ballads*, by John A. and Alan Lomax, published by The Macmillan Company, 1938 • FRED MUELLER, INC. for permission to use pictures from a catalog of western gear • S. D. MYRES SADDLE COMPANY for permission to use cuts from their catalog of saddles • THE PALOMINO HORSE ASSOCIATION for permission to quote in the article on "Palomino" the official description of the Palomino • RINEHART & COMPANY, INC. for permission to quote in the articles "Alkali" and "Squaw Man" from *We Pointed Them North*, by E. C. Abbot. Published by Farrar and Rinehart, 1939 • *The Western Horseman* and WAYNE GARD for permission to quote from an article appearing in *The Western Horseman* and quoting from an original manuscript, "Sketch of Col. John C. Hays, Texas Ranger," by John C. Caperton, 1840.

AUTHOR'S ACKNOWLEDGMENTS

Among the many persons who have been helpful in the preparation of this work the author wishes to thank especially the following:

JERRY ARMSTRONG, rodeo editor, *The Western Horseman*, Colorado Springs, Colorado
WILLARD M. BEAULAND, executive secretary, The Palomino Horse Association, Reseda, Calif.
ROBERT M. DENHARDT, editor, *The Western Horseman*, Colorado Springs, Colorado
WILLIAM H. DEPPERMAN, Steve Hannagan account executive for Winchester Repeating Arms Company, New York City
JOE DE YONG, artist, author, and technical advisor for western movies, Hollywood, California
J. FRANK DOBIE, author, Austin, Texas
J. E. DOHERTY, sales manager, Fred Mueller, Inc., Denver, Colorado
J. E. DRAPER, publisher, *The Horse Lover*, Richmond, California
FRANCIS HAINES, president, The Appaloosa Horse Club, Lewiston, Idaho
L. H. HAMLEY, president, Hamley & Company, Pendleton, Oregon
WRIGHT HOWES, authority on Americana, Chicago, Illinois
MRS. PETER MILLER, owner of the Arabian Horse Farm, Peru, Illinois
S. D. ("TIO SAM") MYRES, president, S. D. Myres Saddle Company, El Paso, Texas
WALTER C. NYE, executive secretary, the Dude Ranchers' Association, Austin, Texas
L. H. RUTTER, postmaster, Hinsdale, Montana
DUFF SEVERE, Severe Brothers, Pendleton, Oregon

For Gordon

INTRODUCTION

ONCE, years ago, while I was walking down New York's Bowery, I saw a secondhand store window filled with cowboy gear. There was a large Stetson hat with a brightly colored horsehair band, a pair of spurs with danglers and four-inch rowels, a braided rawhide rope, a rawhide quirt, a pair of cuffs, a buckskin vest, and many other objects which caused the heart of a true Westerner to beat a little faster.

Then there was a small library—oh, a dozen or more books, some by Emerson Hough, some by Alfred Henry Lewis, and others, too, but all of them about the West and the cowboy. Some real cowboy must have come to New York, gone broke, and been forced to sell all these personal articles. At least, that was the way I saw it. I bought everything I could afford—but particularly the books.

There was hardly a page in these books which did not carry a pasted clipping about the old West or a portion of a letter from some friend in answer to a query on some detail concerning six-guns or rifles, horses, cattle, or individuals of the old western days, or some scribbled note.

For instance, in Lewis' *Wolfville* and *Wolfville Days*, this former cowboy—for he could have been nothing else—had written, "This is a true story. I knew this man"; "A Sharps, not a Winchester, fires this load"; and "Now as regards Road Runners and Rattlers . . ." He had corrected items about the number of grains of powder in a buffalo gun's ammunition. And on the frontispiece of *Wolfville,* under the picture of a stagecoach he had scrawled, "For some reason unknown, Frederic Remington could never draw a stagecoach correctly." It was Lewis' "Old Cattleman" come to life for me!

I still have these books. The owner's name was written in them, but I could never find him to return them to him. In a way they were his own individual "Cowboy Encyclopedia." And his notations caused me to wonder! If one cowboy could find so many things to comment upon in a dozen books on the West, perhaps there were other things about the West—both the old West and the present-day West—which would interest many people. And so the idea of a cowboy encyclopedia was born.

The cowboy and the great cattle empire of which he was a part gave us a true American tradition—the tradition of the West. When the cowboy is introduced, he "snakes" into the picture with the business end of his lariat the old western bad man, the Injun, the cattle rustler, the stagecoach robber, the cattle king, the rattlesnake, the nester, the tenderfoot, the longhorn, the pinto pony, the six-gun and the carbine, the loafer wolf and the coyote, the sagebrush and the cactus, the howling of the norther, the stampede, the creaking of saddle leather and the jingle-jangle of spurs and the chirping of the taster on the horse's bit.

He brings along his lingo, his songs, and his peculiarities of manner and dress. All sorts of men changed into cowboys. But once a cowboy, a man never changed into anything else. The cowboy was different from other people, and while his work with cows and horses was just plain hard labor, he had a certain pride and haughtiness, and he lived by an unwritten code which set him apart from ordinary folk.

The secret of his attitude was that the cowboy rode a horse. To gallop across the immensity of the Great Plains gave him an exaggerated feeling of mastery over destiny. The horse does strange things to the man who rides him. General Paez, in far-away Venezuela, once remarked: "There is no sane man on a horse."

We will not go that far, but will hold to the cowboy's sayings. He said, "A man on foot is no man at all." He claimed, "A man is no better than his horse," and there was a deep philosophy in "You ride the horse and not the saddle."

The word "cowboy" originated in Texas. But in the early days this word meant just about the same as the later term, "cattle rustler." Texans, known as "cowboys," raided Mexican ranches and drove off the cattle. Some of the cattle were sold in New Orleans markets; others used to stock ranges along the coast.

The word dropped out of use for a time, and the men working with cattle in the dense chaparral and thorny thickets became known as "brushpoppers." Later they went by the term "cowhands." When the great cattle herds began to move up the Texas Trail in the 1860's, the drivers were called "cowboys." This time the name stuck. Other names came, like cowpuncher, cowpoke, puncher, and waddie, but the name cowboy fitted these men and was never discarded.

The cowboy of the old days was a hired hand on horseback who worked with cattle and horses. He was a mixture of the riding and shooting frontiersman of the South, the Mexican-Indian horseback worker with livestock, known as the *vaquero,* and the Spanish open-range rancher.

In California there was another type of man who rode and worked with cows and horses. He was the "buckaroo," who got his name from the Mexican word *vaquero*. He did not go by the name of cowboy, but if defined was called a "sporty cowboy."

The influence of the Texas cowboy and the California buckaroo spread beyond their own sections. The Texas cowboy was known by the erect manner in which he rode, his feet straight down in the stirrups, his body making a straight line. The California buckaroo reared back a little in his saddle, his legs thrust forward. The Texan's saddle was rim-fire, or rigged with two cinchas; he was a tie-man, that is, he made the end of his rope fast to his saddle horn; he used a hard-twist manila, maguey, or other fibrous rope; his saddle had a low horn; his bridle usually was plain without a noseband and had a slit in the top of the headstall which fitted over one or both of the horse's ears; and his reins were open at the saddle end. The Californian's saddle was center-fire, or rigged with only one cincha; his rope was the reata, braided from rawhide strings; he was a dally-man, that is, he "dallied," or gave several turns of his rope around his saddle horn which was wrapped with rawhide; his bridle was ornate and decorated with silver conchas; his bridle reins were closed, and attached to them at the saddle end was a long, flexible quirt called a romal.

The influence of the Texan spread north to Canada, and that of the Californian east through Oregon, Idaho, and other western states. There was almost a dividing line at Utah between these two types of hired riders who worked with cows and horses. Where the dividing line came there was a sort of blending between the Californian and the Texan.

But the Californian and the Texan had one thing in common. This was the Spanish or Mexican influence. After more than one hundred years of occupation of Texas and almost that length of time in other parts of the Southwest, the Spanish-Mexican gave the cowboy and buckaroo most of their words for gear, cattle, and horses, and all things having to do with them. But the cowboy promptly said the words in his own way. He called a *fiador* a "Theodore"; a *jáquima* became a "hackamore"; a *mecate* was termed a "McCarty"; a *lazo* was "lasso," and so on. The cowboy, in turn, has handed down such common expressions as "bawling out," "earmarked," "shavetail," and "rough rider."

In THE COWBOY ENCYCLOPEDIA I have tried to bring together the most important and interesting facts about cowboys. Some of the colorful and exciting customs of the "old days" described here are no longer practiced. Yet the cowboy undoubtedly is more popular today than at any time in history. Some enthusiasts may misrepresent or slightly overdo him; but, movie hero or dude ranch roughneck, he is still carrying on the great tradition of the West and Southwest.

Evanston, Illinois
September 24, 1950   BRUCE GRANT

When my old soul hunts range and rest
Beyond the last divide,
Just plant me on some strip of West
That's sunny, lone, and wide.
Let cattle rub my headstone round,
And coyotes wail their kin,
Let hosses come and paw the mound,
But don't you fence it in.

—*Cowboy Songs and Other Frontier Ballads*,
by John A. and Alan Lomax.

THE COWBOY ENCYCLOPEDIA

Aboard. Cowboy term for being mounted on his horse. The cowboy in several instances adopted sea-going terms, as when aboard a bucking horse, he sometimes spoke of being on the "hurricane deck."

Adios (ah-dee-ose'). The Spanish term for "good-by." The cowboy used it as "so long" or "see you later." Like the French "adieu," it literally means "to God."

Adobe (ah-doh'bee). The Spanish word for clay. In the Southwest it is a term for sundried brick as well as for the house of which they are built, and the word is contracted to 'dobe (doh'bee). These houses, with their thick walls, are cool in summer and warm in winter. Adobe houses were built by the Indians of Mexico and Peru, and the early Spaniards adopted this method when they settled in what are now the southwestern states of the United States. American pioneers in Texas, New Mexico, Arizona, and southern California also built 'dobe houses, and they are popular in improved form today.

Airtights. Any kind of canned goods, but particularly canned peaches. Canned tomatoes are considered a good thirst quencher. Sometimes the cowboy carries canned milk which he calls "Contented Cow." Even if a cow is within three feet of him he will do without milk in his coffee rather than milk a cow. The only time he stoops to this low form of life is during a "wild-cow milking contest" in a rodeo. See ALKALI, RODEO.

Alamo (al'a-moh). The battle cry of the old-time cowboy of the Southwest was "Remember the Alamo!" The Alamo, a fort in San Antonio de Bexar (old name for San Antonio), fell to the Mexicans less than six months after Texas declared its independence from Mexico in 1835. Colonel Barrett Travis had 144 men with him in the Alamo when Antonio de Santa Ana and 4,000 Mexicans sat down before it on February 23, 1836, and demanded an unconditional surrender. Travis replied with a cannon shot and the enemy hoisted the red flag, signifying "no quarter." Five days later a courier got through the Mexican lines carrying a message from Travis which has been considered one of the most inspiring messages in American history. It was addressed "To the People of Texas & all

Americans in the world," and said: "I have sustained a continual Bombardment & cannonade for 24 hours & have not lost a man. The enemy has demanded a surrender at discretion, otherwise, the garrison are to be put to the sword . . . if the fort is taken—I have answered the demand with a cannon shot & our flag still waves proudly from the wall. *I shall never surrender or retreat. Then,* I call on you in the name of Liberty, of patriotism & everything dear to the American character, to come to our aid with all dispatch. The enemy is receiving reinforcements daily & will no doubt increase to three or four thousand in four or five days. If this is neglected, I am determined to sustain myself as long as possible . . . . VICTORY OR DEATH."

But no aid came from Sam Houston, to whom the message was sent. Day by day the little garrison held out, some dying from wounds and others from sickness. Thirty-two Texans tried to reach them but were driven back by the Mexicans. Before the garrison was taken, Santa Ana saw a thousand of his men shot down by the Texas sharpshooters. When he finally took the fort he found Travis dead at his post.

Colonel James Bowie, sick in bed, had killed five Mexicans with his rifle and famous Bowie knife. Only David Crockett

and five others were alive. Santa Ana with his own sword struck down Crockett, and the others also were killed, although they were prisoners of war. Not a man survived, and today on the spot in San Antonio where the Alamo stands is a monument with the magnificent inscription: "Thermopylae had its messenger of defeat; the Alamo had none."

Alfalfa. A clover-like plant of the bean family which is considered one of the finest foods for cattle. It is said to have been brought to Mexico by the early Spaniards from the Mediterranean area. The word alfalfa, which is from the Arabic, means "the best fodder." It has been cultivated in the United States since the middle of the last century. In Europe the plant is known as "lucerne."

Alforja (al-for'hah). Spanish for saddlebag or knapsack. It was a wide leather or canvas bag in which the old-time cowboy carried his "plunder," or personal effects, on a pack animal. He pronounced the word "alforge," "allforche," "alforki," or "alforka." See PANNIER.

Alkali (al'ka-lye). A mineral found in the soil, especially in desert regions, which sometimes whitens the ground at the surface. Too much alkali in water poisons it for man and beast. Teddy Blue Abbott, driving a herd up the Texas Trail in 1879, told how they came to a small lake after being two days without water. He described it as "about six inches deep, swimming with polliwogs, and coffee-colored with alkali. We strained out the polliwogs through a handkerchief and tried to drink it. The alkali was so strong we couldn't keep it on our stomachs."[1] The horses drank some of it and the cowboys took off their clothes and rolled around in the water, which seemed to help their thirst.

Alkali dust opens bleeding cuts on the face. Old-time cowboys rubbed canned tomatoes on the cuts and also on the lips of the horses after they had drunk the water.

Ambushing. See BUSHWHACKING.

Angle-Iron. A triangle made of iron which rings loudly when struck. It hangs near the kitchen of the ranch house and is

used to announce meals. While striking it the cook usually shouts, "Chuck! Come and get it!"

Antelope. A prong-horned, deer-like animal halfway between cattle and goats, native to the western plains. The Plains Indians called antelopes "white flanks."

[1] From *We Pointed Them North* by E. C. Abbott. Published by Farrar and Rinehart, 1939.

Their coarse, brittle hair was used for pillow stuffing, the tanned skin for moccasins, and the shinbone was made into a pipe. At certain seasons the meat is very tasty.

The cowboy learned from the Indians to cook the brains by roasting the entire head (after breaking off the horns). Cowboys also took pride in vests made of antelope skin.

Apache (a-pach'ee). One of the Plains tribes of Indians who formerly roamed the desert lands of the Southwest. This territory was called "Apache country." The cowboy considered the Apache a "bad Injun." Apaches were naturally lazy but very active in theft and murder, to which, as one writer said, "they are trained by their mothers, and in which they display . . . cunning, treachery, and cruelty." They were masters in ambushing an enemy and knew the art of concealing themselves. An Apache could look like a granite boulder, for instance, by covering himself with a gray blanket and artistically sprinkling dirt over it. He could disguise himself as a yucca tree, and a cowboy would ride right into what he thought was an innocent bunch of trees only to find himself surrounded by Apaches. These Indians attacked only when confident of success. See INDIANS.

Aparejo (ah-par-ay′ho). Spanish for packsaddle. See PACKSADDLE.

Appaloosa (ap-a-loo′sa). Formerly, the war horse of the Nez Percé Indians of the Palouse country in Washington. The word Appaloosa grew out of Palouse.

One type of Appaloosa is white or cream colored, completely covered with egg-shaped, diamond-shaped, or circular spots, which may be black, brown, or auburn. This is the "leopard" type, sometimes called "polka dot." The other type is a horse with solid-colored foreparts but with hips covered with whitish spots or flecks. This is called the "blanket-hip" pattern. These horses are fine and sturdy and highly prized by cowboys.

The Nez Percé Indians lost their horses in 1877 when the United States seized their territory in Oregon, Washington, and Idaho. More than 800 horses were shot and some 1,100 driven off. Many horses were later found by western plainsmen and recognized as the horses from the Palouse country. It appeared at one time that this type of horse would entirely disappear, but in recent years breeders have been able to maintain and even to increase this strain. See HORSE.

Arabian. The oldest and purest breed of horse in the world. The Arabian horse is important to the cowboy as the ancestor

of the cow pony. The first Arabians were brought to North America by Hernando Cortes in 1520, when he invaded Mexico.

Through hundreds of years the Arabian was carefully nurtured, and is said to have been the first horse to whom an intelligent breeding program was applied. There are 5,000 registered Arabian horses in the United States today. They are not spotted horses, as some believe, but are of solid colors or dappled. It is interesting that the purebred Arabian today has in many cases taken the place of the cow pony, and is used by the cowboy as a stock horse and cutting horse. See HORSE.

Arapaho (a-rap′a-ho). One of the Plains tribes of Indians ranging in southeastern Wyoming and eastern Colorado. Cowboys thought of the Arapahoes as "good Injuns." The men were intelligent and brave and the women virtuous and handsome. Many white men, including Kit Carson, married Arapaho maidens. The Arapaho is always associated with the Cheyenne, and both belong to the Algonkin family. White men first came across the

Arapahoes among the Black Hills in South Dakota, but by 1840 they had moved farther west. In wars against the white man the Arapahoes fought with the Cheyenne and the Sioux. See CHEYENNE, INDIAN.

Armadillo (ahr-ma-dil'o). A small animal with an armor-like covering. It usually comes out only at night. The armadillo, as found in the Southwest, lives on roots, insects, worms, reptiles, and dead animals. Despite his short legs he can run fast, and often tries to escape by burrowing in the ground. He is harmless and does not put up a fight when captured.

Arrow. The old-time cowboy would rather be wounded with a bullet than with an Indian arrow, for an arrow might be poisoned. Some Indians poisoned their arrows by dipping the heads in a compound made from powdered ants mixed with the spleen of an animal and allowed to decay in the sun. A scratch meant death.

Many times the Indian made his war arrow with a head that came off in the wound when the shaft was withdrawn. In attacking blockades and wagon trains, Indians often used fire arrows which would start a blaze. Most arrowheads were fashioned from hoop iron, and by their shape and length a cowboy could tell the tribe to which they belonged.

Arroyo (ar-roy'-o). A small stream or its dry bed. *Arroyo*, in Spanish, means "brook." In the Southwest many areas are cut up by arroyos, which are deep gullies in which water flows only during the wet seasons. See COULEE.

Association Saddle. A standard saddle for saddle-bronc riding in rodeos. The rodeo cowboys formerly made their own saddles, and some of them were wonderful to behold. One old-timer in looking at a saddle said: "That's not a saddle—that's a four-door sedan." Finally the rodeo managers wanted a standard saddle. Hamley & Company perfected one which met with the managers' approval and it became known as the "Association saddle." It has a five-inch cantle and a fourteen-inch swell fork. See RODEO, SADDLE.

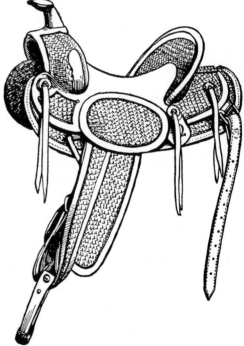

Auguring. A cowboy term meaning talking big. The cowboy sometimes says "the Big Augur" when he refers to the Big Boss.

Bad Lands. A term applied to broken country with deep ravines, bluffs, and hills. During the time of early French explorations the name *mauvaises terres à traverser* (bad lands to travel over) was given to certain sections in Nebraska and North and South Dakota. Thus came the name "Bad Lands." The Bad Lands area of South Dakota is between the White River and the south fork of the Cheyenne River. This was once fairly level plain country, but streams have cut out great ravines and ridges, leaving in many places slender columns of clay which rise like giant toadstools. The Bad Lands of North Dakota along the Missouri River were rolling plains at one time, but are now slashed by ravines whose walls of soft earth have crumbled into fantastic forms.

Bad Man. Outlaws, desperadoes, killers, road agents, and train robbers were called "bad men" in the old West. There have been bad men among all races of people—white, yellow, and black. But the one that topped them all was the white bad man of wild and woolly West.

Every section had its bad man. These men seemed to have been born bad. They were known and feared as killers; they were quick on the draw and were dead shots. They were not thought of as brave, and the ends of many bad men showed them to be cowards. They held up trains, rustled cattle, and took sides—for pay—in some of the bloody cattle wars. Most of them died with their boots on—either shot down or swung from a rope over a limb. Honest men always had friends remove their boots before they died so it couldn't be said they had "died with their boots on," which would put them in the class of desperate bad men.

Some of the worst of the bad men were William R. (Billy the Kid) Bonney, the Younger brothers, Bob and Emmett Dalton, Jesse James, Sam Bass, Big Harpe and Little Harpe, Henry Plummer, Clay Allison, Ben Thompson, Boone Helm, John Wesley Hardin, John Ringo, and Joseph A. Slade. Today these one-time bad men often turn up in movies and books as heroes and Robin Hoods, but in real life they were not so regarded.

The real bad man had others to fear besides the officers of the law. When a bad man gained a reputation as a killer he was always in danger of his life from some upstart who would kill him to gain a reputation for himself. By the code of the West the killer of a bad man "inherited" the notches on the bad man's gun.

Most bad men were members of gangs and had hide-outs in the mountain regions. Some bad men were made town marshals and sheriffs, and once on the side of the law, they usually did their work well. See BASS, BONNEY, GUNMAN, QUICK-DRAW, RUSTLER, TOWN MARSHAL, TWO-GUN MAN.

Balance. The way a horse handles his own weight and that of his rider is called "balance." A horse also is said to have balance when he is well-formed in all his parts.

Band. The old-time cowboy spoke of a "band" of horses, never a "herd" of horses.

He said "herd" of cattle. However, while he "drove" or "punched" cattle he always "herded" horses. See HERD.

Bandanna. See NECKERCHIEF.

Barbecue. A feast at which a beef or other large animal is broiled or roasted whole. A barbecue in the Southwest is a social event. A great pit or ditch is dug and a fire built on the bottom. The beef or other animal is placed over the live coals, supported by green sticks. As the meat cooks it is sopped over with a sauce. This "sop" is composed of vinegar, cooking oil, salt and pepper, and whatever other seasoning the cook wants to add. The meat is served in large chunks right off the carcass.

Barbed Wire. Fence wire, termed "bob-wire" by the cowboy, made of several strands twisted together with sharp spikes fastened into the strands. These spikes are necessary in the West as cattle will rub against smooth wire and loosen it and pull the posts out. But cattle will not go near barbed wire if they can help it, and the only time it will not stop them is during a stampede.

The United States is the home of barbed-wire manufacture. Patents were taken out almost at the same time by Lucien B. Smith, of Kent, Ohio, and William B. Hunt of Scott, N. Y., in 1867. A year later Michael Kelly, of New York, also took out a patent. The coming of barbed wire, which made it possible to keep cattle enclosed, did away with the great roundups of former days. One of the jobs most hated by cowboys is "ridin' fence" and repairing barbed wire. They feel it is a laborer's job. See OPEN RANGE, RIDING FENCE.

Bass, Sam. A Texas outlaw. Although a bad character, Sam Bass became the hero of young Texans, and the song that was sung about him was said to have had a very soothing effect on restless longhorn cattle. He went from Indiana to Denton, Texas, in 1870. There he worked as a handy man for the sheriff and later bought a race horse, the celebrated "Denton mare," which he named Ginny in honor of the sheriff's daughter. This mare beat all the other horses who ran against her, and Sam took her into Mexico. Finally he sold his race horse after some shady races in Mexico, and he and a partner helped drive a herd of cattle to Kansas. Although the herd did not belong to them they sold it, spent all the money, and then began robbing stage-coaches. Sam was a crack shot, carried two guns, and could write his initials on a tree trunk while riding his horse by on a run.

With four companions, Sam Bass embarked on a career of violence that made him feared throughout the Southwest. He was finally shot down in Round Rock, Texas, and is buried in the cemetery there. His sister set up a headstone for him, which reads as follows:

SAM BASS
BORN JULY 21, 1851 — DIED JULY 21, 1878
A BRAVE MAN REPOSES IN DEATH HERE
WHY WAS HE NOT TRUE?

Bawl. The noise made by a bucking bronco was called "bawling" by cowboys. Later they used the term among themselves and "bawled out" anyone whose actions did not please them.

Bay. A red-brown horse. This is claimed by some to be the natural and perfect color of the horse.

Bayo Coyote (bay'o kye'oht). Term for a horse of a dun or grayish-brown color with a black stripe down his back.

Bear Sign. Cowboy term for a doughnut.

Bedding Ground. Also called "bed ground." This was the place along the trail where cowboys bedded their cattle for the night. See NIGHT HERDING.

Beef Herd. For a cowboy, a herd of cattle made up entirely of steers was called a "beef herd." See HERD, STEER.

Bell Mares. In the old West, faithful old mares used in remudas or pack trains. The other horses always followed them. At night the mares sometimes wore a bell so the cowboy could tell where the horses were. See REMUDA.

Belt. A band of leather worn around the waist and fastened with a buckle. In the early days the cowboy's belt was used for

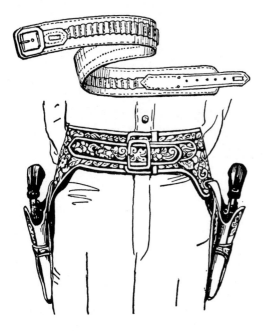

supporting his pistol holster and carrying his ammunition, rather than for keeping his pants up. He either wore no belt for this latter purpose or wound around his waist a bright red Mexican sash or *faja* (fah'hah). Suspenders or galluses were not popular as they got in the way when the cowboy was on a bucking horse.

The proper belt for a holster was about two and a half inches wide and had loops sewed on for carrying extra cartridges. These belts were plain or decorated with carved work and metal conchas. The pistol belt was worn loose, so the weight of the gun and ammunition rested on the hip. A two-gun man might wear a "buscadero belt," which supported two pistol holsters. Another type was a very wide belt which was known as a "kidney belt," and was worn as a support for the back. Today there are a variety of fancy belts with silver buckles, loops, and tips. See BUSCADERO, LEATHER.

Bible Two. A term used by Texas Rangers for the list of fugitive bad men published every year by the Adjutant General's Office. It was almost as religiously read by the Rangers as Bible One, or the Holy Book. At one time it was said that the Texas Rangers had a list of 5,000 desperadoes who were wanted by the law.

Big Horn. A Rocky Mountain sheep which has very large horns. These animals are found in the roughest sections of the mountains and are very sure-footed and

agile. They are khaki-colored with white hips. The long, curved horns are prized as decorations in ranch houses.

Big Swimming. Certain wide, treacherous streams were called "big swimming," but this term was usually applied to streams which had flooded and so made it hard for animals to swim across.

Billy the Kid. See BONNEY, WILLIAM F.

Bit. The metal part of a bridle which goes into the horse's mouth and to which the headstall and reins are attached. The center bar of the bit which connects the two side pieces, or "cheeks," is known as the "mouth," or "mouthpiece." When this center bar is joined or linked together in the middle, the bit is called a "snaffle bit." When the bar is curved or looped upwards, this loop is called the "port." Inside this port

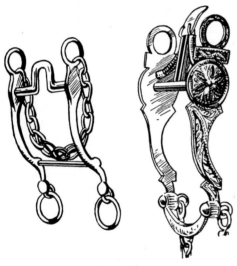

OPEN PORT BIT   SPADE BIT

may be a small wheel or roller called a "barrel roller." The horse likes to spin this with his tongue. In the Mexican or Spanish bits this roller sometimes is of copper and is termed a "taster." Horses like to taste it, and when it spins over it gives off a chirping sound which delights both the horse and the rider. Cowboys riding alone love

the creaking of leather, the chirping of the taster, and the jingle-jangle of their spurs. The side pieces, or cheeks of the bit, have rings on the upper and lower ends. The reins are fastened to the lower rings and the "head" or headstall to the upper ones.

There are many kinds of bits and as many kinds of arguments as to which is the best. One type is called a "spade bit." It has a flat metal projection on top of the port which presses against the roof of the horse's mouth when he is reined in. In a bad rider's hands this is a cruel bit and may cut the horse's mouth, but it is a good bit for experts. When such a bit is used there are buttons or fancy knots along the reins, not as decorations but as weights to balance the bit.

A "curb bit" has a small strap, braided or plain, or a chain which rests under the lower end of the horse's jaw in the chin groove. When the reins are pulled this strap or chain presses against the horse's jaw.

There are also "half-breed bits" in which the lower part of the port is closed; "spoon spade bits" with a spoon-shaped piece of metal on top of the port; and "hackamore bits." These last-named bits do not have the metal bar or mouthpiece.

Some bits are very fancy and are made of silver with gold inlay, and are engraved. These usually have a decorated bottom bar as well as silver conchas on the sides. These conchas, being hollow, make the sound of the spinning barrel roller louder and, some cowboys say, "more pleasin'." See BRIDLE, CONCHA, HACKAMORE, HEADSTALL, REINS.

Bit Hole. A space in a horse's mouth between the front and back teeth where the mouthpiece of the bit fits. See BIT.

Bitter End. The end of a cowboy's rope opposite the honda, or loop end. The rope is hung on the right side of the saddle, the honda end in a large loop with the honda forward, and the "bitter end" to the rear. To tail off the end of the rope, it is sometimes back-braided and other times finished off with a Turk's-head knot so the strands will not unravel. When a cowboy's rope reaches the end and is not tied to his horn he is in a bad way, and this has given rise to such everyday expressions as "to the bitter end" or "at the end of his rope." See HONDA, ROPE.

Blab. This is a device used to wean calves on the range. A thin board or piece of tin,

six by eight inches in size, is clipped into the calf's nose. This does not prevent him from grazing, but does prevent him from getting close enough to his mother to nurse.

Black Jack. A kind of scrub oak which is hard and tough. It is found in the West and Southwest. "Black jack country" is the name applied to that section originally occupied by the Cheyenne and Arapaho Indians. General John J. Pershing's nickname, "Black Jack," given him while he served on the Border, was probably derived from this same tree.

Black Snake. This is a name for both a kind of snake and a whip. The snake is long and black and cowboys think a lot of him because he can kill a rattlesnake.

A black-snake whip is a heavy whip made

of leather or rawhide, the handle filled with lead, shot, or a piece of iron.

Blemish. A scar or other defect which a horse gets through an accident or otherwise. A blemish does not affect the soundness of a horse. It may be only a small cut. Some "sorry-lookin' critter" with a lot of blemishes may be the cowboy's best horse.

Blind. A piece of leather or a folded bandanna which is placed over a raw bronc's eyes when the bronco buster mounts. The cowboy removes it after he is in the saddle. See BUST.

Blind Post Office. A crevice in a rock or trunk of a tree where news items and letters are exchanged. Often used in early days by outlaws and cattle rustlers, but also used today by cowboys.

Blind Trap. A trap corral used in the old days to catch mustangs, or wild horses. It had long wings on either side and was camouflaged with branches of trees and

grass, as wild horses would not go near wire if they could see it. See CORRAL, MUSTANG, WATER-HOLE TRAP.

Blizzard. A high wind accompanied by a blinding snow. One of the hardest jobs of the cowboy is getting cattle to cover during a blizzard, or as it is termed in Texas, a "norther." The natural tendency of cattle is to drift before a blizzard, staggering blindly along with the wind until it stops. If the cowboy cannot turn them back or get them behind the protection of trees, high rocks, or into sheltered valleys, he has to remain with the herd. In the days of the open range, cattle might drift as far as a hundred miles from their home range. Even if they seek shelter the cowboy has to see that they do not get into box canyons or gorges where high snow might pile across the open end and trap them. See Box Canyon, Drift.

Blotching. To erase a brand with a hot iron. This was a trick used by cattle rustlers. A large scar resulted over the original brand so that it could not be used to prove ownership. See Rustler.

Blow Up. See Bucking.

Blue Jeans. See Levi's.

Blue Joint. See Grass.

Bobcat. A wildcat or bobtailed cat. This animal is found in various sections of the United States, and is called by different names in different parts of the country. In the Southwest it is termed "bobcat," "wildcat," and "catamount" (cat of the mountain). In the Dakotas and Canada it is called "lynx." In other places it is spoken of as "cougar" and "puma."

Cowboys sometimes have fun roping these fierce animals, but they are sure they get two ropes around a bobcat so he "can't crawl up one" and attack the roper. Bobcats attack horses and other animals by dropping on their backs from trees. The cowboy believes this is why an untamed horse bucks when a man tries to ride him. As this was the only way wild horses could get bobcats and other wild animals off their backs, bucking became a sort of instinct. See Bucking.

Bonney, William F. (Billy the Kid). One of the worst of the western bad men. Billy the Kid was born in New York on November 23, 1859. His family later moved to Coffeyville, Kansas, where his father died. At the age of twelve the Kid killed a man in a saloon brawl. Then with a companion he went to Arizona. While stealing horses from the Comanche Indians he killed three Indians. During a gambling argument he killed a white man and then fled to Mexico. Here he killed a Mexican in a gambling house and began a career of robbing monte games. He killed one monte dealer whom he waylaid.

He went to New Mexico and became engaged in the Lincoln County War there. His killings mounted. Finally he was sentenced to hang at Lincoln on May 13, 1881, but escaped, killing two guards. After he killed an agency clerk on government property, Pat Garrett, sheriff of Lincoln County, went after him. Garrett killed the Kid in

the home of a friend where he was hiding out. In all, the Kid was said to have killed twenty-one men, "not including Mexicans and Indians." He was five feet seven, weighed 135 pounds, had blue eyes with curious hazel spots in them, and was a hard

rider and a crack shot. At times he was generous and made friends easily. In recent years attempts have been made to picture the Kid as a wronged man and a hero, but in the old days he was known as a ruthless killer. See Bad Man.

Bootblack Cowpuncher. A man who came from the East to go into the cattle business for what money there was in it.

Boot Hill Cemetery. The graveyard in the old "Cowboy Capitol," Dodge City, Kansas, where many men were "buried with their boots on." The term was applied to almost any burying-ground for "bad men." See Bad Man.

Boots. The cowboy's boots are his pride and joy as well as his "safety-first." He insists on boots being handmade and does not want "store boots." While he likes them fancy, all this fancy business has a practical purpose in his work.

The high, undercut heels are to keep his feet from slipping through the stirrups if he is thrown. To have the foot caught in a stirrup is called being "hung up," and being hung up is the cowboy's nightmare. Most cowboys like to ride with the foot well "home" in the stirrup, instead of resting on the ball of the foot. The narrow heel and underslope of the boot make it easier to free the foot quickly from the stirrup, and also give the spur a better chance of pulling off if caught. The boot top is loose, too, so that the boot can slip off the foot if the cowboy is hung up. A tight, laced boot would not come off.

When the cowboy is roping on foot the high heels dig into the ground and give him a better footing. The toe of the boot is pointed to make it easier to pick up the stirrup when a horse is frisky, and to find the right-hand stirrup when the cowboy hits the saddle. The high tops protect the legs from mesquite thorns, brush, stirrup leathers, and even snakes.

If a boot is repaired it must be full-soled, not half-soled, as the edge of the half sole might catch in the stirrup. And as for all the fancy stitching, it helps stiffen the leather. Stitching on the toe gives the illusion of a smaller foot—and the cowboy is very vain, usually wearing boots a size too small for comfort. Cowboy boots are not made for walking, and there is no sadder sight than to see a cowboy limping toward his ranch house after his horse has thrown him or gone off and left him. He is "plumb like a fish out of water."

Boots today are different from those worn by the early cowboys. The tops of the old-time boots came almost to the knee, but when cowboys began to wear chaps the boot tops became lower. See Hung Up.

Boots (Horse). A leather shield worn on the lower part of a horse's leg for protection when a horse "interferes" or strikes his adjoining legs while in motion.

Border Shift. Tossing the six-gun from one hand to the other so it would "come down shootin'." This was sometimes necessary when the gun-hand had been injured and the gun had to be switched to the other hand. It was also a form of exercise or training so the cowboy could develop rhythm, balance, and timing. See Pistol.

Bosal (boh'zal). The noseband of a hackamore. The bosal (from the Spanish *bozal*) is used in place of a bit. It goes around the horse's nose, and when the reins, which are attached to the heel knot of the bosal, are pulled, the horse's wind is closed off and he comes to a stop. Bosals are usually braided from rawhide over a twisted rawhide core. Modern bosals have a steel cable for a core.

The use of the hackamore with bosal is one of the oldest ways of breaking a horse. It is still a favorite method in California today. The headstall of the hackamore is attached to the sides of the bosal. See Hackamore, Mecate.

Bow. An Indian weapon. Even when the Plains Indians carried rifles or carbines they usually had a bow and a quiver well filled with arrows. The Indian's gun might get out of order, he might run out of ammunition or it might get wet, but his bow was always ready for use. Until the invention of the breechloader, it was a fact well known in the West that the bow was a more deadly weapon at close range than the best rifle. The Indian warrior could discharge his arrows with more speed and accuracy than the most expert plainsman could charge and fire his muzzle-loading rifle.

Bowie Knife. A sheath knife, usually with a blade nine inches long, which was made famous by Colonel James Bowie of Mississippi. The story is that the knife was invented by a Negro blacksmith named

Manuel, who worked on the plantation of Rezin P. Bowie, a brother of James Bowie, in Louisiana. Manuel one day fashioned the knife with its peculiar point sharpened on both edges, from a large file. It had a length of fifteen inches with the handle. James Bowie, when he first saw it, liked it and took it with him to New Orleans where it attracted the attention of experts. George Wilkins Kendall, then editor of the *New Orleans Picayune*, wrote an article about the knife and printed a picture of it.

Bowie, thinking the knife could be improved upon, gave an order to a knife-maker named Pedro, who made up one that was lighter and keener, with a thinner blade and a longer point. This was the model of the Bowie knife which later became so famed. Up and down the Mississippi and throughout the South no southern gentleman was considered armed unless he had a Bowie knife within reach. The original knife, made from the file by Manuel, was lost in the ashes of the "big house" on the plantation when it was burned by Federal soldiers. Colonel Bowie fell with David Crockett and other daring spirits at the Alamo. The "Pedro knife" of Colonel Bowie was carried away by the Mexicans.

The fame of the knife lived on, and for years no cowboy would be without one. Some state laws forbade the selling or carrying of a Bowie knife, but manufacturers merely put the same knife out under other names. When the Indian-fighting times were over the cowboy stopped carrying long knives except when hunting. Today he is content with a heavy jackknife or claspknife.

Box Canyon. A deep gorge or ravine with steep sides and one end closed. See BLIZZARD.

Brahma Bull. The toughest, fiercest type of bull used for rodeo bulldogging contests. Next to the old longhorns, the

Brahma cattle are considered the wildest-natured animals the range has ever known.

They have many longhorn characteristics, being docile one minute and ready to stampede the next. However, the Brahma is said to be the only cow that can stage a stampede by itself. The first Brahmas were landed in South Carolina from India in 1848. In the early eighties they began to enter Texas and have since become a very popular breed along the Gulf Coast.

Brand Blotter. A cattle or horse thief who blotted out a brand by running a hot iron over it. Only a large scar was left instead of the original brand. See RUSTLER.

Branding Iron. An iron used for burning brands on the hides and skins of animals. There are two types of branding irons,

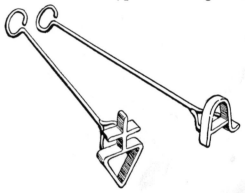

the "running iron" and the "stamp iron." The running iron is a metal rod, like a poker, and is used like a pencil to "write" the brand on. The stamp iron is in the form of a block of type or is made into the design of the brand. The branding iron is heated a cherry red before being applied.

The running iron was much used by cattle rustlers, and in some states there was a law against carrying one. Cattle thieves then used metal rings, horseshoes, sidebars of riding bits, and sometimes bailing wire or telegraph wire, which could be concealed in pockets or saddlebags. See BRANDS, RUSTLER.

Brands. Marks of ownership upon the skin or hide of a living animal made with a hot iron, or some other means. Branding cattle became necessary in the old days when there were no fences and the cattle grazed on the open range. The brand was the owner's trade-mark. Horses were branded, too.

During the big roundups cattlemen had representatives to sort out their own brands, and later, when the cattlemen's associations were formed, inspectors were placed at loading points and brands on all cattle noted. On finding other owners' brands among the cattle, the inspector credited them to the rightful owners, despite the fact they were shipped by the rancher who was selling them. This shipper later would settle with the owners. Too many strange brands in a herd of cattle made the inspector suspicious and he would ask questions. He would consider the cattle stolen unless ownership was proved. All brands at this time were registered with the cattlemen's association, or at county seats.

When using a branding iron, cowboys spoke of "running a brand." The spot where the brand was placed was important. Different owners might use the same brand but each would put his brand on a different place. The letter B, for instance, might be used by several cowmen, but one would burn it in one spot and another in a different spot. Also, the same brand could be placed on the same spot, but in different positions—such as the letter A, which could be standing straight, or lying on its side, or slanted. It would be called Big A, Lazy A, or Rocking A, according to its position. In selecting his brand the cowman tried to choose one which could not be altered by cattle thieves. These "brand artists" could, by use of the running iron, easily change a C into an O or a circle. The letter I could be changed into one of twelve other letters;

a numeral 3 into an 8 or a B; and so on.

A "fast brand" was an honest brand and was burned deep. A "slow brand" was burned lightly, and later a rustler could put his own brand over it. This was also known as the "hair brand" because it merely burned the hair off. These dishonest brands were made at a roundup when the rustler and the cowboys who were doing the branding were working together.

As it was illegal in some states to have a branding bonfire outside of a corral, and a man caught with a running iron was arrested, many times a rustler would just pull the hairs out of a cow in the form of a brand and later catch this cow and slap on his own brand. By using a damp sack, piece of buckskin, or saddle-blanket, and branding through it with a hot iron, a rustler could make a brand that looked as if it had been made some time ago.

A cowboy was supposed to be able to read brands and tell whether they had been tampered with. Brands with squares around them were known as "boxed brands"; those without as "open brands." A ring was called a Circle. A dash was a Bar. Capital letters were known as Big. As an example of how brands were read, the brand A-10 was called A-Bar-Ten. Horses usually were branded only once, and if sold the buyer relied on his bill of sale to prove ownership. Cattle, however, were branded as often as sold. The seller would "vent" or cancel his old brand by running a line through it and then placing on the buyer's brand.

Besides branding with a hot iron, there were other types of branding. The "broken bow brand" was made by the use of notches, sawed at the base of a two-or-three-months old calf's horns, which caused the horns to grow in a distinctive downward direction. The "dewlap brand" was made by cutting a flap of skin on the breast or brisket of a cow and letting it hang. The

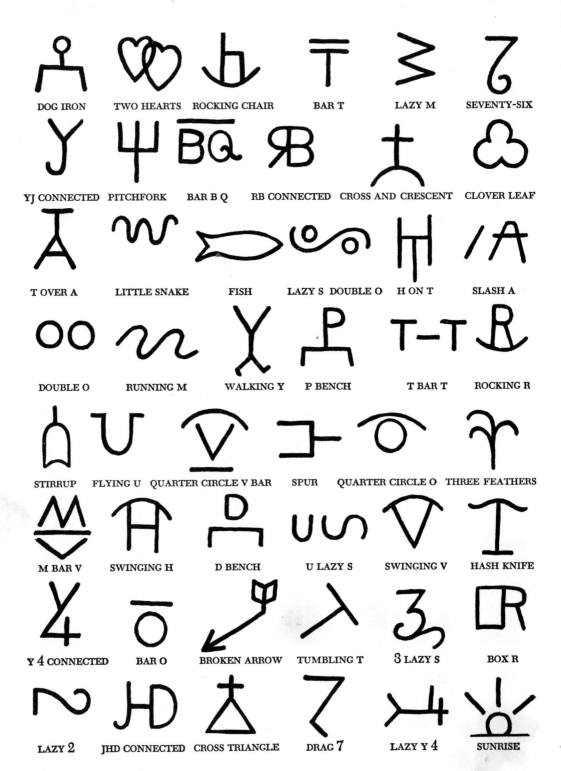

DOG IRON   TWO HEARTS   ROCKING CHAIR   BAR T   LAZY M   SEVENTY-SIX

YJ CONNECTED   PITCHFORK   BAR B Q   RB CONNECTED   CROSS AND CRESCENT   CLOVER LEAF

T OVER A   LITTLE SNAKE   FISH   LAZY S DOUBLE O   H ON T   SLASH A

DOUBLE O   RUNNING M   WALKING Y   P BENCH   T BAR T   ROCKING R

STIRRUP   FLYING U   QUARTER CIRCLE V BAR   SPUR   QUARTER CIRCLE O   THREE FEATHERS

M BAR V   SWINGING H   D BENCH   U LAZY S   SWINGING V   HASH KNIFE

Y 4 CONNECTED   BAR O   BROKEN ARROW   TUMBLING T   3 LAZY S   BOX R

LAZY 2   JHD CONNECTED   CROSS TRIANGLE   DRAG 7   LAZY Y 4   SUNRISE "wattle brand" was similar, except that the flap was cut on the jaw, neck, or nose of the animal. A "jug-handle brand" was similar to the dewlap brand, but the flap of skin was slit and a piece of rope or wire put in so that when it healed it would have a round hole in it. The "jingle-bob brand" was made by deeply slitting an ear so that it would droop.

There was a large variety of earmarks, made either with a knife or a punch, and sometimes cows were both branded with a hot iron and marked with the knife. In knife marking there were cuts known as "overslope," "underslope," "crop," "half crop," "overslit," "underslit," "upperbit," and "underbit." See EARMARK, MAVERICK, RUSTLER.

Break. See BUST, GENTLING, INDIAN-GENTLED.

Breakaway Roping. A rodeo type of roping which originated in Texas. The rope end is tied to the saddle horn with a string, and when the roped calf breaks the string the judge lowers his flag. This is faster than roping a calf and then tying him.

Breast Collar. A wide strap in a horse's harness which passes around his breast. Usually a saddle breast collar is highly ornamented and is more for show than use. However, it does keep the saddle from slipping back.

Breeching. A wide strap in a horse's harness which passes around the rump.

Bridle. The head harness of a horse which consists of the headstall, bit, and reins. The headstall alone is sometimes called a bridle. The headstall and reins of a bridle usually match. If the headstall is braided the reins also are braided. In the

fancier bridles where the bits are decorated with conchas or other ornaments, this decoration may also appear on the headstall. See BIT, HEADSTALL, REINS.

Bridle-wise. A term used when a horse has learned to respond to the bridle and particularly to the bit. Usually, though, a cowboy guides his horse almost without use of the bit. A slight pressure of the left rein against the horse's neck will turn him to the right, and the rein against the right side of the neck will turn him to the left. A touch of the hand or leg on the animal's hind leg will cause him to turn, also. Pushed on the right side the horse will turn right, and on the left side he will turn left. To increase his horse's gait, the cowboy leans slightly forward and lifts the reins; to stop him he pulls lightly on the reins and says, "Whoa," at the same time lifting his right hand in the position of throwing a rope. The bit in a horse's mouth is there for punishment, and the horse soon learns this. See BIT, REINS.

Bronco. A small, wiry, spirited horse. A "raw bronco" is an unbroken horse. The cowboy usually shortens the word to "bronc." *Bronco* in Spanish means "rough" or "wild." See BRONCO BUSTER, BUST.

Bronco Buster. The term for a cowboy who breaks or "busts" a horse. The old-time bronco buster did little else but break horses. He went from ranch to ranch and charged five dollars for every horse he busted. He was known as a "rough rider," "bronc-peeler," "bronc-twister," or a "contract buster." In this rough business a man was usually so "wore out" or badly injured after a few years that he had to take on easier work. Emerson Hough said of such men, "Sometimes their lungs were torn loose by the violent jolting of the stiff-legged bounds of the wild beasts they rode, and many busters would spit blood after a few months at their calling."[1] See BUST.

Broomtail. Wild or range mares. Sometimes called "broomies." See FUZZTAIL, MUSTANG.

Brushing. When a horse strikes his adjoining feet while in motion, he is said to be "brushing."

Brushpoppers. The name given to the early type of southwestern cowboy. He "popped" longhorn cattle out of the brush and chaparral where they would hide. See CHAPARRAL, COWBOY, *Introduction*.

Buckaroo. The old California term for cowhand or cowboy. He was a man who could bust a bronc or punch cattle. As he went in for fancy Spanish gear he was sometimes called a "sporty cowboy" or a "high-loping cowboy." The word buckaroo came from the Spanish *vaquero* (vah-kay'-ro). The B and V in Spanish sound alike.

Buckboard. A four-wheeled vehicle with long, springy boards resting on the axletrees, instead of steel springs. It was for-

[1] From *Story of the Cowboy*, by Emerson Hough. Published by Appleton-Century-Crofts, Inc., 1897.

merly a familiar sight around a ranch, used for trips to town for mail and supplies. The automobile station wagon has taken its place today.

Buck Hook. A blunt-nosed, up-curved hook on the top of a spur shank which enables a rider to "lock" his spurs in the cinch or in the side of a horse when it is plunging. See SPUR.

Buckhorn. See CACTUS.

Bucking. The act of a horse in plunging up and down with arched back and rigid legs in an attempt to unseat his rider. It is the natural instinct of the horse to buck, as this is the way his ancestors rid themselves of wild animals that attacked them by jumping on their backs.

Bucking or buck-jumping, as they say in the North, is the same as pitching or the old Texas expression "cayusing," terms used in the Southwest. An honest bucker is the delight of the cowboy. If a raw bronc fails to buck when first ridden the cowboy is suspicious of him, and he usually turns out to be a "spoiled horse" that can never be depended upon.

In order to buck, a horse must have his head well down between his legs; so from the time he mounts, the rider tries to keep the horse's head up. In straight-away bucking the horse leaps up and down, first with his fore feet and then with his rear feet off the ground. When he looks like a drowned cat held up by the middle of the back, with all four feet off the ground, he gets the hearty applause of the "chute roosters" and others on the sidelines. These horses will probably buck about five seconds and then quiet down. An ordinary bronco buster does not have much trouble staying on their backs.

But the kinds that are hard to ride are those that start out bucking as though they were leaping to the time of an Indian's war drum and soothe the cowboy into thinking he is riding a roller-coaster; then suddenly change their dance step by twisting and turning like an athletic jitterbug in a soda parlor. These are called "gizzard poppers" and "gut twisters," and the cowboy needs plenty of "glue on his pants" to stick on. The best riders are those who figure out just what a horse is going to do next and "roll with the punch" like a boxer, or get into position to take the shock before it comes.

will have "a bellyful of bedsprings." They call a horse a "blind bucker" when he becomes so excited that he loses his head and may buck into, over, or through anything. A horse "breaks in two" when he leaps into the air after a short run. The "cat-back" horse is one that does not put much spirit into his bucking, as if his mind were on something else. The cowboy speaks of this type also as "pussy-back," and such a horse may "crow-hop," or be a "goat," and do a "frog-walk," or "sheep jump."

The "close-to-the-ground" bucker is one very quick in his actions, and while he bucks hard he never gets very far off the ground. He kicks to the rear sideways and shakes his head violently. A "high-roller" is a horse that leaps into the air when bucking. He is sometimes called a "high-poler." A horse "lights heavy" when he jumps into the air and comes down stiff-legged. A "pile-driver" is a type that humps his back

DROWNED CAT

SPINNER

Cowboys have more different expressions for describing bucking horses than any other thing. When a horse starts to buck he is said to "blow up." He may also "boil over," "come apart," "kettle," "unwind," "shoot his back," "wrinkle his spine," or "bow up." If he is an unusual bucker he

and comes down with all four legs stiff. Smart cowboys just relax and sit limply in the saddle in such cases. A "spinner" is a horse that bucks in tight circles, turning either to the right or left.

A "sunfisher" is probably the best-known type of hard bucker. In "sunfishing" the horse twists his body into a crescent shape with the head and tail first one way and then the other. He acts as if he were trying to put first one shoulder and then the other on the ground. He is much like a "sunfish out of water," and is one of the toughest types to ride.

The "weaver" is a horse that in bucking never brings his feet down in a straight line, but weaves them in the air before landing. There are also vicious horses called "outlaws" and "killers." They try to bite the rider and sometimes rear and throw themselves backwards. This is dangerous to the rider as the horse may fall on him. See BOBCAT, BUST, GENTLE-BROKE, INDIAN-GENTLED, RODEO, THROW-BACK.

SUNFISHER

Bucking Strap. A strap placed around a horse's belly and pulled tight. This makes him buck and is used on horses in rodeos to increase the excitement. See RODEO.

Buckshot. Leaden balls which come in five different sizes, from about one-fourth inch to one-third inch in diameter.

Buckskin. A soft, tough, and yellowish leather made from the skin of the deer. After the animal is skinned, the skin is first

made into rawhide. Then the brains of the deer are rubbed in, and the skin is worked and pulled and twisted until soft and pliable. It is then sewed into a conical bag and suspended over a small fire of white cedar, red cedar, or oak chips, according to the color desired. The smoke tans the skin, closes the pores and toughens as well as conditions it, so that it will remain soft even after it has been wet. Buckskin is highly prized by cowboys for shirts and vests. Commercial buckskin today is made by an alum-tanning process. See RAWHIDE.

Buck Strap. A loop of leather at the base of the saddle horn used for a handhold when riding a bucking horse. Top (expert) riders never use it.

Buck Tie. A method of tying up a prisoner in the old West. The wrists were lashed together, the hands and arms passed

over the knees and a rifle or stick shoved between the joints of the knees and elbows.

Buffalo. The American bison. At one time these animals roamed the plains by the millions. The Indians believed the buffalo was made for them by the Creator. The Cheyenne and Arapahoes had a religious superstition that each year thousands of buffaloes poured out of two great holes on the Staked Plains, south of the Canadian and east of the Pecos rivers. The Indian made use of practically every part of the buffalo—skin, bones, flesh, and sinews—for food and clothing.

The cowboy, though, considered the buffalo a menace. A herd of buffaloes would stampede a herd of cattle, and in many cases the cattle would join the buffaloes. In some cases a herd of buffaloes would attack both cattle and cowboys. But while the buffaloes roamed the prairies, wolves and other wild animals left the cattle alone, and the Indians liked buffalo meat better than cow meat.

When the buffaloes were killed off by professional buffalo hunters to provide food for the thousands of workers on the Union Pacific and the Northern Pacific while these railroads were being built across the cattle country, wolves and Indians both began to raid cattle herds. Indians became even more resentful when pleasure hunters came West and killed buffaloes for sport—or simply for the delicacy of buffalo tongue. The great herds began to disappear as professional "skinners" swarmed the plains and killed the buffaloes only for their hides. These were followed by "bone pickers," who carted away the bones and sold them for fertilizer. When there were no more buffaloes and no more bones, these men turned to cattle rustling. So the cowboy had little use for the buffalo, dead or alive.

The buffalo has not altogether disappeared. The latest count by the Department of the Interior shows 2,800 in the United States. However, instead of encouraging an increase in the buffalo population, the government now aims at keeping the herds within limits established by range conditions.

There is a herd of 1,300 buffalo at Elk Island National Park, Alberta, Canada. The average yearly increase there is about two hundred, and control of the herd is maintained by supervised slaughter every two years. See BUFFALO SKINNERS, INDIAN, STAMPEDE.

Buffalo. To confuse. When a cowboy is "plumb buffaloed" he is too puzzled to know what to do.

Buffalo Bill. See CODY, WILLIAM F.

Buffalo Gun. A rifle or carbine of .50 caliber, known as the 50-120, used for killing buffalo. It could be also a rifle of .45 caliber. See CARTRIDGE, RIFLE.

Buffalo Skinners. Men who made a business of killing the buffaloes for their hides. A complete "outfit" of buffalo skinners consisted of seven men, two to kill the buffaloes, four to skin them, and one to cook. See BUFFALO.

Buffalo Soldier. An Indian name for Negro soldiers. Their woolly heads reminded the western Indians of the curly fronts of the buffalo bull. Indians would not scalp a buffalo soldier as they considered it "bad medicine."

Bulldogging. Throwing a steer or bull by leaping on its back and twisting the head around by using the horns. The animal has to be going at full speed so it can

of case, bullet, powder, and primer. Nor is bullet the same as ball, which is a round projectile larger than shot. See BUCKSHOT, CARTRIDGE.

Bull Rigging. A broad strap or rope which passes around an animal's body and to which are attached hand holds. It is used in wild-steer riding in rodeos. See RODEO.

easily be thrown off its balance. Throwing steers by "bulldogging" was formerly done sometimes at branding time, and it is now a favorite event in the rodeo. See RODEO.

Bullet. The metal projectile which comes out of a rifle or pistol when fired. A bullet cannot be called a cartridge, which is a complete round of ammunition consisting

Bull-Whackers. Teamsters who trained, yoked, and day after day walked alongside the oxen which pulled the heavy freighters of the ox trains across the prairies. They carried long rawhide whips with which they drove their teams and with which they could kill rattlesnakes along the way. They were considered a tough bunch, but many employers made them sign agreements "to abstain from treating their oxen cruelly, from gambling, from getting drunk, from using profane language, and from doing anything incompatible with the conduct of a gentleman." They were paid one dollar a day and expenses. See Bull Whip.

Bull Whip. A whip with a short stock which was weighted with lead. The lash of the whip, from fifteen to twenty-five feet in length, was braided rawhide and tapered to a point to which was attached a buckskin "popper" about three feet in length. This whip was used by bull-whackers, or drivers of ox teams. With the popper they could make the whip crack like a pistol shot, and by a mere flip remove four square inches of an animal's hide, or snap the head off a rattlesnake. See Bull-Whackers.

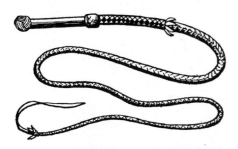

Burro. A small donkey used in the mountain sections of the West as a pack animal. The burro can carry a heavy load, is sure-footed in rough country, and is able to stand hunger and thirst. Burros are tough and stubborn and frequently balk like mules. To make them move, once they decide to remain in one spot, is difficult. Whipping, beating, or pulling at their halters does not budge them. The old-timer, however, knows that if he acts indifferent and just turns and walks away, tugging at the lead rope, the burro will follow. It is said a burro will not move as long as a man looks him in the eye.

In the Rocky Mountain section the burro

is called the "Rocky Mountain canary" because of his very "melodious hee-haw." Ranchers, knowing that wolves love burro

meat better than that of any other animal, use it as bait, tying to it little packages of strychnine done up in cigarette paper. In Spanish, *burro* (boo'r-ro) means a donkey or ass as well as "stupid fellow." See Pack Horse, Wolfer.

Buscadero. Another name for an outlaw or "long rider." A "buscadero belt" is one from which two guns can be hung. See Bad Man, Belt.

Bushwhacking. The shooting of unsuspecting or helpless victims; sometimes also called "dry-gulching." Bushwacking was a little different from ambushing and could mean sneaking up and shooting a man.

Bust. To break or gentle a horse for riding. The cowboy's idea is to make the horse understand from the very start the superiority of the man. When the horse is roped he is sometimes tied up and allowed to run against the rope, thus learning to respect its strength. Later, the minute a rope falls around a horse's neck, he stops still. Then the cowboy introduces him to the hackamore. The horse wears this until he realizes that when he tries to bolt away the bosal on the hackamore closes off his wind. Next a saddle is placed on him, and he is allowed to buck to his heart's content until he sees

he cannot dislodge it. Finally the rider mounts. Every time the horse bucks he feels the spur and the quirt. After being ridden several times the horse comes to know that any time he acts up he will feel pain. Some old-time cowboys tried to "break the heart" of a bronco, but most ranchers did not tolerate cruelty. This did not mean, though, that a rider should let a horse "get away with anything." The so-called "pet horse" or "spoiled horse" was and is considered the most treacherous of animals. See BRONCO BUSTER, BUCKING, INDIAN-GENTLED.

"Bust" also means to jerk down violently. To "bust" a roped animal is to throw him down. In the rodeo if a calf runs against the rope and "busts" himself it is all right, but if the rider busts him he is penalized twenty seconds. See RODEO.

Button. A term used by cowboys to mean the Turk's-head or woven leather and rawhide knots on their quirts and bridle reins. One section of a rattlesnake's rattlers is also known as a button. See LEATHER BRAIDING, QUIRT, RATTLESNAKE.

Cabestro (cah-bes′tro). A rope made of horsehair and used mainly for tying.

Cactus. A desert or prairie plant generally covered with sharp stickers or thorns, common throughout the Southwest. There are many kinds and varieties of cacti, but the most common is the prickly pear. The fruit of this plant is called "tuna," or Indian fig. Cabeza de Vaca, an early explorer who was captured by the coastal Indians of Texas, tells in his *Narrative* how the Indians took the ripe fruit, squeezed the juice into a hole in the ground, and then drank it. The prickly pear is admired for its beautiful yellow and reddish-yellow blossoms. During droughts ranchmen singe off the thorns, using a flame-throwing machine carried by a man on foot and fed by a small portable tank. Cattle then eat the plant. It was said the old-time longhorns could go for days without water by eating the prickly pear. It is upon this plant that the tiny insect, the cochineal, feeds. The Aztec Indians made their famous dyes from the cochineal.

The buckhorn is another common type of cactus with branches like the antlers of a deer. The cholla (choh′ya), or giant cactus, is said to have more thorns to the square inch than any other variety. The spines are so fine that they look like silvery down. Another type is the hedge-hog cactus, with several hundred varieties. It is barrel-shaped or cone-shaped with ridges like a melon and is covered with large thorns. Cowboys use the thorns as toothpicks. Mescal (mays′kahl) is a spineless cactus which the Mexicans use to make their intoxicating drink of the same name.

The thorns of most cacti have barbs like fishhooks, and once embedded in the skin begin to work beneath it. Cowboys usually carry a small piece of thin, square-edged metal which they use to pull out cactus thorns. They catch the end of the thorn between the metal and thumb. The back of a knife blade is sometimes used for the same purpose.

Calaboose (kal′a-boose). The cowboy's word for jail. It comes from the Spanish *calabozo* (kal-a-boh′tho), meaning dungeon. See HOOSEGOW.

Caliber. The diameter of the bore of a rifle or pistol. This is measured from the inside of the barrel before the rifling grooves are cut. Caliber is not the same as gauge. See GAUGE, PISTOL, RIFLE.

Calico Horse. The popularity of spotted calico in the West inspired the name of "calico horse" or "calico pony" for an animal with all-over spots. See PINTO.

A cowboy also sometimes spoke of a woman as a "calico," because in the old West women wore calico more than any other material.

California Sorrel. Another and older name for Palomino. See PALOMINO.

Canteen. A metal bottle covered with felt and used for carrying water. The water can be cooled by wetting the outside covering. Other types of canteens are made of

coated canvas and leather. They are hung from the saddle horn, and are necessary items in the cowboy's equipment.

Canter. A slow gallop. See GAIT.

Cantineses. See SADDLE POCKETS.

Cantle. The up-curved back part of a saddle. See SADDLE.

Carbine. A rifle having a barrel much shorter than standard, usually intended for use on horseback. It was formerly carried in a quiver-shaped, open-mouthed scabbard, and the carbine was usually slung, butt forward, in an almost horizontal posi-

tion on the left side, the scabbard passing through the two leaves of the stirrup leather. Old-time cowboys rarely used the word, but called the weapons rifles. See RIFLE.

Cartridge. A complete round of ammunition for a rifled firearm. The cartridges of the cowboy were of two types. One was the "rim-fire," in which the priming was contained inside the folded rim of the cartridge and would explode when the hammer struck any part of the rim. These were the old-time rifle cartridges. The other type was the "center-fire," in which the priming was encased in the center of the "head" of the metal case. The rear end of the cartridge was the "head," the "case" contained the powder charge, and the projectile was called the "bullet."

Early center-fire cartridges were identified by three hyphenated numbers, as 45-70-500. This meant .45 caliber with 70 grains of black powder and a bullet weighing 500 grains. When Winchester brought out his Model 73 in 1873 it was built for a center-fire cartridge. The same year Colt chambered his famous six-shooter to carry the same ammunition. The cartridge was designated as 44-40 (.44 caliber and 40 grains of powder) and could be used in either rifle or pistol. Thus the cowboy carried only one type of ammunition for both. The bullet weighed 200 grains.

A cartridge for a buffalo gun was 50-120-550; that is, .50 caliber, 120 grains of powder, and 550-grain bullet. The cartridge for the old needle gun had a paper case, and the primer was in front of the powder charge. See BUFFALO GUN, BULLET, COLT, NEEDLE GUN, PISTOL, RIFLE, WINCHESTER.

Cat. Cats were highly prized on ranches. The standard price for kitty throughout the cow country was $10 in the old days. As food usually was laid in for a year, cats were necessary as mice and rat catchers.

Catch Rope. The cowboy's working rope or lariat. See ROPE.

Cattalo (cat'a-lo). A hybrid breed of cattle produced by crossing a cow with a buffalo. This was done by C. J. ("Buffalo") Jones, ranchman and author of *Life on the Plains*. The breeding experiments have been successfully carried out by the Canadian government at the great Buffalo Park near Wainwright, Alberta, Canada. In the breeding, Hereford, Shorthorn, or Aberdeen-Angus cows have been mated with purebred American bison.

The hide of the cattalo is similar to that of the buffalo in quality. The hair is thick and the robe has great warmth. The cattalo is a rugged animal and fitted to weather the terrific gales of the Medicine Hat region. Such cattle face the storms instead of drifting with them, a great advantage. They are able to thrive on pasture that might mean starvation for the domestic cow, and during winter they muzzle down through the snow and get feed. They do not require shelter.

Cattle. The cattle of the West originally came from Mexico. They were the longhorn type, or Andalusian cattle which had been brought into Mexico as early as 1519 by the Spanish conquerors. When Mexican settlers moved northward over the Rio Grande River into Texas, they lived on large *haciendas* and their cattle grazed on the open range. There was no market for cattle, and as the herds increased many wandered off and became wild. These cattle seldom went beyond what is today northern Texas.

In 1821, when people from the eastern and midwestern states began to settle in Texas, they found great herds of wild cattle. They captured many and learned from the Mexicans how to brand and mark them. These animals were the beginnings of the great southwestern herds. Years later Devon, Hereford, and Shorthorn cattle were imported into the Southwest to breed out the longhorn variety and produce cattle which were bigger and better for the eastern markets. The longhorn gradually disappeared and today only a few are left.

The cattle of the Northwest were of a different type. Tame cattle from the eastern farms were brought out and turned loose on the plains.

To the cowboy, a member of the cattle family is always born a "calf." After a year the male becomes either a "bull" or a "yearling." The bull is thereafter known as a

CALF

"two-year-old bull," a "three-year-old bull," and so on. On his second birthday the "yearling" becomes a "steer." Two years later he is known as a "beef." The female calf becomes a "heifer" on her first birthday, or a "young cow." Then she is a "two-year-old cow," a "three-year-old cow," and on her fourth birthday becomes a "beef." The general term for female cattle is "she stock," but there is no such thing as "he stock." "Feeders" are cattle which are being fattened before selling, and "stockers" are those placed on an unoccupied range. But the cowboy rarely uses the term "cattle." He always says "cows" if he is talking about cattle. See Cow, LONGHORN.

Cattle Drive. The term used for driving great herds of cattle up the trails from the open range to the shipping points. The trail herds, averaging 3,000 cattle, usually were made up of cattle from various ranches. As they bore different brands, they were first "road-branded," that is, a light brand was placed on all of them.

The herd was in charge of a "trail boss." The second in charge was the "straw boss" or "segundo." There was one cowboy to every 250 to 350 cattle, depending on the type of country to be passed over. A cook who drove the chuck wagon and prepared the meals, and a "remuda man" or "cavvy-rango" who had charge of the extra horses, completed the crew. Each cowboy had from five to nine extra horses in the remuda.

When the herd started moving, cowboys rode on each side of it, about two hundred yards apart. Those in front on each side were lead riders or "point men." The next were "swing riders" or "flank riders," and bringing up the rear, behind the herd, were the "drag men" or "tail riders." A scout rode ahead almost a day's journey to look for water and safe fords.

When the herd started there was always a scramble among the strongest animals to gain the lead. Finally one steer or cow would assume this place and would keep at the head of the herd throughout the drive. Each day, no matter how badly they had been scrambled during the night, each animal took the same position in the herd that he had first taken. The herd moved from sunup until late afternoon, making from ten to fifteen miles a day. At night the cattle lay down and slept, while night herders rode around them, singing and whistling to keep them quiet.

The cowboy was always alert for any signs of restlessness which might mean a stampede. Herds of buffaloes, bands of unfriendly Indians, and swollen streams were other dangers. If no danger threatened, the drive was merely a long, dusty journey.

The herds rarely exceeded 3,000 head, because of the difficulty of watering them. When cattle after a long and dusty march came near water, they all rushed to it at once. A herd of 3,000 would line a river bank for a mile, and unless they had plenty of room the weaker ones would be trampled to death. See CATTLE TRAILS, NIGHT HERDING, STAMPEDE.

Cattle King. A cowman or rancher who owns great tracts of grazing lands and thousands of cattle. The term was first given these fabulously wealthy men by easterners in the late 1870's when the cattle business was at its height. They also were called "cattle barons," and the cattle business was spoken of as the "beef bonanza." The whole country was excited over what was considered an easy way to become rich through cattle raising and trading. This was about the time that the English invested considerable capital in western cattle-raising companies.

The cattle king deserved his name, even though it was never to his democratic liking. These men ruled over vast empires, some of which are in existence today. Among those still operating is the great King Ranch in southeastern Texas, the largest in the world, which consists of 1,250,000 acres. Captain Richard King laid the foundation for this empire in 1851 when he acquired the Santa Gertrudis ranch of 65,000 acres, with headquarters at Kingsville, Texas. The King Ranch is so huge that there is a month's difference in

crops of the north and south sections. Crossing its farflung acres is a journey. One traveler put it this way in verse:

"The sun's done riz and the sun's done set

An' I ain't offen the King Ranch yet."

The ranch has its own representative in the United States Congress and ships an average of 17,000 cattle to market every year.

John W. Iliff became known as the "Cattle King of Colorado." Miller & Lux on the West Coast had ranches from Southern California to Oregon and into Nevada. John Chisum controlled a great section in the Pecos Valley and was known as the "Cattle King of New Mexico." Charles Goodnight first saw the possibilities of raising cattle on the Staked Plains and his cattle ranged the Palo Duro Canyon.

Though in later years syndicates bought many of the great ranches, cattle kings still reign and are scattered throughout the West and Southwest. See BRANDS, CATTLE, OPEN RANGE.

Cattle Trails. More than 5,000,000 cattle thundered up the great cattle trails from Texas to the shipping points in the North during the years 1867 to 1884. It was the largest cattle movement in the history of the world, and the route over which the herds were driven was called the Texas Trail. Someone said: "The Texas Trail was no mere cowpath. It was the course of an empire." The War between the States was over, the Indian uprisings had been put down in the Southwest, and the railroads were pushing westward. When the Kansas Pacific Railroad was completed at Abilene, Kansas, in 1867, 35,000 cattle came into that cow town during the summer.

From many points in Texas paths and trails came together, leading from ranches and cattle ranges, and then flowed northward into one great highway. One route,

the Fort Griffin and Dodge City Trail, began at Bandera, Texas, near San Antonio, and went due north about 600 miles. This passed through Fort Griffin and crossed

the Red River at Doan's Store in the Indian Territory (now Oklahoma). The herds swam the Washita, Canadian, and Cimarron rivers. The Arkansas River was crossed at Dodge City, the end of the trail. The trunk trail through the Indian Territory was known as the Chisholm Trail.

Other routes were started in order to skirt the newly settled sections. The Old Shawnee Trail, after running parallel to the Chisholm Trail for 100 miles, veered east to strike Baxter Springs in Kansas. Where this trail touched the Canadian River, the Middle or West Shawnee Trail began its course to Junction City, Kansas. Still another trail was the West Chisholm Trail, sometimes called the Ellsworth Cattle Trail, which entered western Kansas at Ellsworth. To the west was the Pecos Trail, with paths from the west and southwest meeting at Horsehead Crossing of the Pecos River, and between this and the Chisholm Trail was the Panhandle Trail, perhaps the hardest of the drives as it touched the unwatered tablelands of the Llano Estacado (Staked Plains). See Cattle Drive, Chisholm Trail, Cow Towns.

Caviada (kah-vee-ah′dah). A group of saddle horses. In the Southwest they also used the terms "cavvy" and "cavvieyard." These were the cowboy's pronunciations of the Spanish term *caballada* (cah-bah-lyah′-dah), meaning a group of horses. The term "remuda" was used in the North. See Remuda.

Cavvieyah (kav′ee-yah). The cowboy's way of pronouncing the Spanish word *caballo* (kah-bah′lyoh), meaning horse.

Cayuse (kye-yuse′). The name of an Indian tribe in Oregon, also used to denote an Indian pony. It came to be used loosely throughout the North and Northwest to mean any kind of bronc or small horse.

In Texas the term meant "a pitchin′ or buckin′ hoss." For "pitching" Texans said "cayusing." See Bucking.

Chaparral (chap-ar-ral′). From the Spanish word meaning a dense thicket of thorny brush or dwarf trees. The chaparral is to be found in the Southwest, and in

the early days was a favorite hiding place for the wild longhorn cattle. See Brushpoppers, Cow Hunt, Longhorn, Mossy Horn.

Chaps. A pair of leather leggings with wide flaps, worn by the cowboy to protect his legs. The term is an abbreviation of the Spanish *chaparejos* (chah-pah-ray′hos), meaning leather leggings. Chaps are held up by a belt which is usually highly decorated with silver conchas and fancy carved or stamped work, and laced together with a thin lacing which will easily break if a cowboy gets "hung up" or caught on his saddle when thrown.

Chaps are worn as armor for the legs while riding through sagebrush, cactus, or chaparral. They are protection when a horse tries to bite the rider or brushes him against a fence or other animal, or when a rider is thrown or a horse falls on him. They are shields against rain and snow. "Shotgun chaps," worn in Nevada and California, have decorative fringe sewed in the side seams. "Bat-wing chaps" have extra large flaps and are fastened on the sides with rings and snaps. These are considered very showy and are used today by movie cowboys. "Angora chaps" are made of sheepskin, with the wool or hair outside. Hides of other animals with the fur

45

or hair left on are also used. They are warm, and the hair sheds the rain and snow. These are worn on the open prairies and in Wyoming and Montana. When different colored fur is sewed in, these are known as "pinto chaps." The so-called "straight-legged chaps" were on the order of the "shotgun chaps" but without the fringe. They were popular in the Southwest.

Chaps were worn by old-time cowboys only when working or when calling on their girls. They figured nothing impressed the womenfolks like chaps, spurs, guns, and fancy belts. These were the cowboy's "Sun-day-go-to-meetin' clothes" which he wore when in "full war paint."

Charro (char'r-ro). The fancy horseman of Mexico. He is a flashy, daredevil rider and fits himself out in the finest clothes and his horse in the finest gear. He is the gentleman *vaquero*.

Cheyenne (shy-en'). Plains Indians belonging to the Algonkin family. The Cheyenne were regarded by old-time cowboys

as "good Injuns," although they were chief among those Indians who fought to the last to keep the white man from advancing his

frontier. The Cheyenne men were brave, and in physique and intellect superior to most Plains Indians. The women were handsome and noted for their virtue. Many white men selected wives from among the Cheyenne.

The Cheyenne Indians were closely allied with the Arapahoes, and like this tribe observed the sun dance ritual. The Cheyenne are believed to have come originally from around the headwaters of the Mississippi River. They later settled in Nebraska, and after they had acquired horses began to hunt buffalo on the plains. They ranged through Kansas, Wyoming, and Colorado.

The Cheyenne fought alongside the Sioux in many battles against white men, and they took part in the Custer Massacre. In 1878, led by Chief Dull Knife, a small band of Cheyenne broke from their reservation in the Indian Territory and in crossing Kansas out-fought and out-maneuvered the best of the United States soldiers before they finally were defeated and surrendered. See ARAPAHO, INDIAN.

46

Chili Con Carne. A spicy Mexican dish which is popular with cowboys. It is made with meat, chili peppers, and frijoles (beans). In the Southwest good chili con carne must also be made with bulls' eyes, which serve as a binder. "Chili mac" is chili with macaroni.

Chinook (chih-nook'). A warm wind that blows from the northwest. Coming in the early spring, it often brings sudden thaws and floods.

Chips. Sun-dried manure left on the range by cattle and buffalo. Both cow chips and buffalo chips were highly prized by the cowboy of the old open range. On the treeless plains he used them as fuel for his campfire. They gave a hot, blue flame.

Chisholm Trail. This famous trail came into being in the year 1867 when the government decided to move more than 3,000 Wichita Indians and affiliated tribes to a reservation in the southern part of the Indian Territory. The Indians were on the Arkansas River near where the Chisholm and Cowskin creeks empty into it. Major Henry Shanklin, in charge of the Indians, made a deal with a wealthy half-breed named Jesse Chisholm to open a trail and establish supply depots along the way through the Indian Territory to the banks of the Red River.

When Jesse Chisholm started out from the Arkansas River with a large train of ox teams, he drove before him a band of one hundred wild horses to settle the quicksands in the Salt Fork, Cimarron, and North and South Canadian rivers. The ponies were driven back and forth over the treacherous quicksands until the terrain was made safe for crossing. The Indians followed later with their thousands of ponies and many mounted soldiers as guards. While passing over the small trail blazed by Chisholm, this large body of Indians and ponies formed a beaten road.

The territory the Indians vacated became the site of Wichita, Kansas, and when the Atchison, Topeka & Santa Fé Railroad was built, this town became a shipping point. Later, when cattle were brought north from Texas, they were driven up until they reached the Chisholm Trail at the Red River.

CATTLE BEING LOADED AT ABILENE

At the Montopolis crossing on the Colorado River, just below Austin, Texas, many small trails from the Gulf Coast merged into the Chisholm Trail, which became a great roadway several hundred yards wide and extending 700 miles to Wichita, Kansas, and on to Abilene, where the Kansas Pacific Railroad touched. The famous cowboy song, "The Old Chisholm Trail," is said to have more than one thousand verses and many versions. Every cowboy who traveled the famous trail added some personal experience. See CATTLE TRAILS, COW TOWNS.

47

Cholla (choh-ya). This name has been given to a new cowboy game popular on the West Coast. The idea of the game is for mounted riders, usually six on a side, to rope the big, six-legged, leather-padded

"jack," similar to the child's toy, from the center of the field, and "snake" it down to the goal posts, thus scoring a point. The name came from the resemblance of the jack to the cholla, or giant cactus.

Chouse (chowse). To punch or drive cattle.

Chuck. Food. The cowboy also speaks of "eats," "chow," and "grub." Sowbelly (bacon), beef, bread, and coffee were the principal foodstuffs of the range in the old days. In the North they used more beans and dried apples. The northern bread was usually made of wheat flour, while in Texas it was made from corn meal. During a roundup a cook might carry along a jug of sour dough for making "risin' bread." Hoe-cake and flapjacks were popular.

The cowboy had to have his coffee, or "Java." In the South it was sweetened with sorghum molasses, in the North with cane sugar. Sometimes a cowboy would have to boil his coffee in the bean:

> *My fire I must kindle with chips gathered round,*
> *And boil my own coffee without being ground.*[1]

[1] From *Cowboy Songs and Other Frontier Ballads,* by John A. and Alan Lomax. The Macmillan Company, 1938.

The cowboy usually put his ground coffee in cold water in the coffeepot, brought it to a boil, and then settled it with a dash of cold water. If he had no coffeepot he might make coffee in the frying pan after he had cooked his bacon. The lone cowboy, too, might cook his bread (flour and water) by rolling the dough around the end of a stick and holding it over the hot coals.

Some of the cowboy's food, like peaches and tomatoes, "growed in cans." If he had milk, that came from a can, too. Eggs were a luxury, and whenever a cowboy went to town he ordered ham and "States' eggs" —the imported egg from the East and the only thing he would admit was better than the western variety. He liked Mexican food, too, his favorites being chili con carne, hot tamales, and enchiladas.

During a roundup, if the cook was in a good humor he might whip up a "son-of-a-gun" stew, into which he put a little of everything. "Salt hoss," or corned beef, was to be had on occasion. When his meal was served the cowboy would fall to at once, or someone might say grace: "Eat your meat and save the skin; turn up your plates and let's begin." See CATTLE DRIVE, CHUCK WAGON, FLAPJACK, HOECAKE, ROUNDUP.

Chuck Wagon. A mess wagon that carried the cooking outfit and food supplies when the cowboys were driving a herd up the trail, or during a roundup. It was the cowboy's "home" when on the open range.

The chuck wagon or trail wagon, or as early Texans called it, the "commissary," followed directly behind the remuda, or band of extra saddle horses. It was an ordinary four-wheeled farm wagon without springs, and on the back part was built a "chuck box," with shelves and drawers for food and cooking utensils. The tail-gate let down on two legs and made a table for the cook's use. When this table was down,

there was kept underneath it a dishpan for dirty dishes, called a "wreck pan." Swinging beneath the wagon was a "cooney," or dried cowhide, to carry firewood or buffalo and cow chips. Inside the wagon was the precious water barrel with a faucet on the side. The "jewelry chest" for storing hobbles, extra ammunition, strips of rawhide for repairs, and other odds and ends, was on the outside near the front.

The chuck wagon was drawn by four horses, mules, or oxen. It carried a month's supply of provisions, as well as the bedding for the men and their extra clothing. The cook, or "cookie," rode the chuck wagon and was lord and master. Sometimes there were added luxuries such as a "bed wagon," driven by a "flunky," which carried the cowboys' bedding, and a "hooligan wagon," which carried only firewood and water. But as a rule the chuck wagon carried all these necessities on the trail. See CATTLE DRIVE, CHUCK, ROUNDUP.

Chute Gate.   The gate leading into the rodeo area or corral. See RODEO.

Chute Roosters.   Rodeo-wise boys who perch on the top of the chutes and know how everything should be done and don't mind telling about it. See RAILBIRD.

Cigarette Rolling.   See "MAKINGS."

Cincha or **Cinch** (sin'cha).   A wide strap or band which goes around the horse's belly to hold the saddle on his back. Each end is fitted with a large metal ring called the "cincha ring." The reason for rings and not buckles is that they make it easier to adjust the latigo or strap within a fraction of an inch. Sometimes a horse will swell up by filling his lungs with air, and after the cincha is fastened he will shrink so that the saddle will be loose and the cowboy will find himself riding beneath the horse in-

stead of on top. The best cinchas are made from soft mohair, and others are of horse-hair and cotton fish line. The word is Spanish. See LATIGO, RIGGING.

Cinch-Binder. The type of horse that rears on his hind legs, loses his balance, and falls backwards. This "fall back" is dreaded by cowboys.

Circle Riders. Cowboys who ride in a large circle during a roundup and drive the cattle to the roundup ground or corral for branding and tallying. See ROUNDUP.

Cody, William Frederick (Buffalo Bill). A famous scout, Indian fighter, and showman. Buffalo Bill was born February 26, 1846, in Scott County, Iowa, near Le Clair. As a youth he was a stagecoach driver and Pony Express rider. In 1863 he joined the 7th Regiment of the Kansas Cavalry and served with this outfit through the War between the States.

In 1867 he made a contract with the Kansas Pacific Railroad to furnish its workmen with buffalo meat. He won his name "Buffalo Bill" when he killed eleven buffalo while hunting with some army officers, and a short time later defended his right to the name by killing sixty-nine buffalo to forty-eight killed by Billy Comstock, chief scout at Fort Wallace, who had challenged him. He was an Army scout in the fights against the Cheyenne and Sioux in 1869, and in 1872 was elected to the house

of representatives of Nebraska. He killed Chief Yellow Hand in single combat while a scout with the United States 5th Cavalry.

In 1883 Buffalo Bill organized his famous Wild West Show, and four years later toured Europe with it. From this time on he was principally a show man. He was a picturesque-looking man and wore his hair long. Indians called him "Pashaska," or "Long-Haired Chief." He died January 10, 1917, at Denver, Colorado. See NEEDLE GUN, PONY EXPRESS.

Collected. A "collected" horse is one that does not "wing" but travels smooth. In the East "collected" means the horse's movement behind the bit and his energy under control. See WINGING.

Colt. A young stallion horse. When under one year he is called a "foal." A female, or young mare, is called a "filly." Cowboys can tell a colt from a filly at a distance. The colt is venturesome and will run toward a man, while the filly will keep close to her mother. See FILLY.

Colt. A type of revolver. Just as a hat in the West was called a "Stetson" and a rifle a "Winchester," a revolver was termed a "Colt." Samuel Colt had got the idea for his revolver in 1829 while on a ship bound for India. He watched the spokes of the ship's wheel turn and lock in position, and the idea occurred to him of making a weapon with chambers which would turn in the same manner, and which could be fired through a single barrel. The name "revolver" came from Colt's Revolving Pistol.

Colt went broke, but some of his revolving pistols had been used by the Texas Rangers and their fire-power was demonstrated on the Texas battlefields. With these "revolvers" the Rangers could fire ten shots to the enemy's one. When the Mexican War began in 1846, Captain Samuel H. Walker of the Texas Rangers went East to persuade Colt to start manufacturing pistols again. He had some suggestions for the improvement of the pistol. Colt went into business once more, and the first thousand pistols turned out were called "Walker Colts." The Rangers meantime had named the pistol a "six-shooter," and so the Colt was called in the West.

During the days of the stagecoach, Colt also made a special .31 caliber revolver known as the "Wells Fargo Colt." This was a five-shot revolver and was used by Wells Fargo & Company messengers.

The first Colts used paper cartridges, but when metallic cartridges came in Colt developed his famous model of 1873, an Army revolver called the "Single-Action Army Revolver," "Frontier Model," or "Peace-Maker." This was the cowboy's gun and his law, and he spoke of carrying "Judge Colt and six provisions of his statutes." Later

Colt chambered this revolver so it would take the same 44-40 ammunition as that used in the Winchester Model 73 rifle. The cowboy then had to carry only one type of ammunition for both. See CARTRIDGE, PISTOL, TEXAS RANGERS, WINCHESTER.

Comanche. A tribe of Plains Indians of the Shoshoni branch of the Uto-Aztecan family. The cowboys considered the Comanches "bad Injuns," and they were Enemy No. 1 of the Texans.

Comanches were excellent horsemen and were known as "horse Indians" as far back as the white man is acquainted with their history. They were close kin to the Kiowas and Snakes, and the three tribes ranged the Great Plains east of the Rockies. The

stamping ground of the Comanches was south and east of the Staked Plains. They had raided Mexican settlements from the earliest days, stealing horses and mules, killing the men and carrying off the women and children. The Texans offered more resistance than the Mexicans had, and there was almost continual warfare between them and the Comanches.

The last outbreak of the Comanches, then confined to a reservation in the Indian Territory, was in 1874 when they killed ninety ranchers and members of their families. These Indians always raided at the time of the full moon, and cowboys on trail or at a ranch were especially alert at such periods. See INDIAN, TEXAS RANGERS.

Come-along Hackamore. A halter made with a lariat looped over the head of the horse, with a half hitch around the nose. When pulled it pinched the horse's nose, and was used in breaking him to lead. See HACKAMORE.

Concha (kon'cha). A silver or metal ornament used on belts, bits, bridles, and saddles. The word is Spanish, meaning "shell." The typical concha is a bulged-out disk of silver engraved or stamped. When used on bits, the conchas serve as decorations as well as to intensify the sound of the "cricket" or "barrel roller" on the mouthpiece of the bit, which the horse rolls with his tongue. See BELT, BIT, BRIDLE, ROSETTE, SADDLE.

Corona (koh-roh'na). A saddle pad. From the Spanish *carona* (kah-roh'nah), meaning that part of the horse's back where the saddle goes. See SADDLE BLANKET.

Corral (kor-ral'). From the Spanish, meaning a fenced yard or enclosure for animals. Each ranch has one or more cor-

rals, which are used chiefly when branding or breaking horses. The large public corrals on the old-time cattle trails, where cowboys could keep their herds at night and get a little rest, were built circular. This was in case of a stampede, so that by yelling and waving their slickers the cowboys could get the cattle milling around in the circular area and exhaust them. In Texas corrals were called "round pens." See BLIND TRAP, CATTLE DRIVE, ROUNDUP, SQUEEZE CHUTE, WATER-HOLE TRAP.

Cottontail. A small, gray rabbit with a white tail. This rabbit is typical of the South and Southwest and is good to eat.

Cottonwood. A species of western poplar tree, so-called because of the white, cottony seeds which fall about the middle of

June each year. The sight of this tree was always a welcome one to the cowboy—it indicated water was near. In winter the bark was good food for horses and cows.

Coulee (koo'lee). A deep gulch, usually dry, with inclined dirt sides. It differs from an arroyo, as the latter is usually the bed of a stream. See ARROYO.

Coupling. That part of the horse which connects the hindquarters with the barrel. If the space between the last rib and the hip is narrow, say three fingers in width or less, the horse is "close-coupled." If the length is greater, he is "long coupled."

Cow. Specifically, a female of the cattle family, two years old or over. But in the old West all cattle were cows. The cattle ranch was the "cow ranch," the cattle country was the "cow country," and a cowboy's horse was a "cow horse." Even cowboys who herded only horses were known as "cowboys." See CATTLE.

Cowboy. One old-timer said a cowboy was "a man with guts and a horse." The cowboy of the old West was a hired hand on horseback who worked with horses and cows. But he would not admit he "worked." He said he "rode for" such and such a "brand" or "ranch." He rode "a ten dollar horse and a forty dollar saddle." But he rarely owned his horse. He furnished his rope, saddle, bridle, and clothing, but he was hired to ride other people's horses.

The cowboy was carefree, ready for anything, never took a dare, was quick to fight when insulted, and never curious about strangers. He was honest, and his word was like a gold bond. Out-smarting Easterners or Englishmen was never considered dishonest. His rope was his third hand. If asked to bring in some wood for the cook he would rope it and "snake" it up to the chuck wagon. He would not stoop to do any kind of laborer's job, nor would he even milk a gentle cow. But dare him to milk a wild one, than which there was nothing more ornery or treacherous, and he would do it or die. He liked to think he could ride "anything with ha'r on." His life was a hard one, yet his sense of humor never left him. A song called "The Cowboy" goes:

"All day on the prairie in a saddle
  I ride,
Not even a dog, boys, to trot by my
  side;
My fire I must kindle with chips gath-
  ered round
And boil my own coffee without be-
  ing ground.
I wash in a pool and I wipe on a sack;
I carry my wardrobe all on my back;
For want of an oven I cook bread in
  a pot,
And sleep on the ground for want of
  a cot." [1]

When he went calling on the girls he dressed in "full war-paint," with spurs jangling, six-gun in his holster, in fancy vest, chaps, boots, and sombrero. He figured nothing impressed the fair ones like spurs, guns, and chaps. When he got "hog-tied" by some female he was no longer a cowboy. He had to become a cowman.

Cowboying. See RAKE.

Cowboy Lingo. One fellow said that cowboy lingo "is perfectly easy to under-

[1] From John A. and Alan Lomax, *op. cit.*

53

stand. All you've got to do is to know in advance what the other fellow means and then pay no attention to what he says."

The cowboy picked up most of the words for his work and his gear from the Mexicans. He got other words and expressions from Indians, and some cowboys in the Northwest used the Chinook slang of the coastal trappers and traders. But the cowboy said everything in his own way. He called the Mexican *fiador* (fee'ah-dohr) on a hackamore a "Theodore," and a *mecate* (may-kah'tay) or hair rope became a "Mc-Carty." Even "hackamore" came from the Mexican *jáquima* (hah'key-mah). The French word *chassé,* meaning a movement in dancing, was called "sashay" and meant a waltzing movement of a horse. *Cayuse,* first the term for an Indian pony, came to mean any small horse. And from gamblers he adapted all sorts of terms like "freeze-out," "bluff," "ante," and "kitty." He would "run a brand" and "top a horse." See CHUCK.

Cowboy Songs. The cowboy ballads have been called the true folk songs of America. The cowboy told his story and that of others in song. He sang to keep from growing lonesome and he also sang to quiet the restless longhorn herds on the trail at night. Cows seemed to like such bedtime stories. One song has it:

> *"What keeps the herd from running,*
> *Stampeding far and wide?*
> *The cowboy's long, low whistle*
> *And singing by their side."*[1]

Trail bosses did not like to hire a rider who could not sing. It did not matter what kind of voice he had, just so he could carry a tune. Songs considered "plumb sooth-in' " to cows included "Sam Bass," "Dim Narrow Trail," and "The Cowboy's Dream." These were favorites on the Chisholm Trail, as well as the song about the

[1] From John A. and Alan Lomax, *op. cit.*

trail itself, "The Old Chisholm Trail."

But cowboys also sang about the little dogies, the bad men, horses, cows, and

about their sweethearts and their old homes. In one song the cowboy says, "Bury Me Out on the Prairie," and in another, "Bury Me Not on the Lone Prairie." But he was agreed on one thing—he didn't want to be fenced in, either when in his grave or on his horse. The deaths of brave cowboys and rangers and the riding of wild broncs gave him other themes for his songs.

One of the best collections of cowboy ballads has been made by John A. and Alan Lomax in *Cowboy Songs and Other Frontier Ballads.* See NIGHT HERDING.

Cowhand. An early name for a cowboy who rode for a ranch. The term "cowboy" did not become general until cattle were driven up the Texas Trail to the northern shipping points. Cowhands were sometimes called "brushpoppers." See BRUSHPOPPER, COWBOY, *Introduction.*

Cow Hunt. This term was used in the West before the word "roundup." The longhorn cattle hid in the chaparral and it was a real hunt to find them and to get them out. See LONGHORN.

Cowman. A ranch owner who raises and sells cows.

Cowpuncher. The cowpuncher originally was a cowboy or other person who punched cows with a long spiked pole when loading them into cattle cars. The name caught on and later was used to mean the same as "cowboy" or "cowhand." A variation of cowpuncher is "cowpoke." See COWBOY, *Introduction.*

Cow Towns. Towns which sprang up along the famous cattle trails, the railroads, and in the cattle country where the chief industry was ranching and cattle raising. Abilene, Kansas, where the Chisholm Trail connected with the Kansas Pacific Railroad, was one of the first, and set the style with its saloons, dance halls, bank, and "New York Store." Dodge City, Kansas, became known as the "Cowboy Capital of the World."

At Abilene the cowboys off the trail were so unruly that such men as William B. (Wild Bill) Hickok, the famous quick-draw and dead-shot marshal, were appointed to keep them in line. In 1872 things became so bad that farmers of Dickinson

County sent a circular to Texas asking the drovers "to seek some other point for shipment, as the inhabitants of Dickinson will no longer submit to the evils of the trade."

Wichita, Kansas; Miles City, Montana; Ogallala, Nebraska; Cheyenne, Wyoming; and Sidney, Nebraska, were a few of the other famous cow towns. See CATTLE DRIVE, CATTLE TRAILS, HICKOK.

Coyote (kye'oht). A small dog-like wolf of the prairies. He lives in a hole which he digs himself. He is a pest and attacks livestock and will dig up corpses of humans when they are not buried deep enough. On moonlight nights he howls at the moon, and cowboys when celebrating like to imitate this howl.

"Coyote" also was the name given to a person of mixed Indian and Mexican blood. One of Indian and Negro blood was a *Meztizo,* and a person of American and Mexican blood was a *Zambo.*

Crease. To cut the cord in a horse's neck with a fired bullet and daze him. This method was used in the olden days for catching mustangs, but it was a very delicate operation. If the bullet went too high it was a miss, and if a fraction of an inch too low it broke the horse's neck. If a cowboy was afoot on the plains and his horse ran away, he would take a desperate chance of creasing him. See MUSTANG.

Critter. Any animal, but used chiefly to mean a cow.

Cross Draw. The act of drawing a pistol with the right hand when it was worn on the left side. The pistol was carried either in the waistband of the trousers or in a holster with the butt of the gun forward. The gunfighter had to cross his arm over to whip it out. When two guns were worn, both with butts forward, the gunfighter employed a "cross-arm draw" to take them out. Carrying a gun in the holster on the left side with the butt forward was the correct position when riding, as the gun was more accessible. See HOLSTER, PISTOL, QUICK-DRAW.

Cross Hobble. A method of hobbling a horse by fastening together a front and a rear leg on opposite sides. See HOBBLES, SIDE-LINING.

Crow Hop. See GAIT.

Cuff. A leather gauntlet which guards the cowboy's wrists and shirtsleeves. Cuffs are usually decorated with conchas and

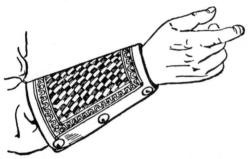

carved or stamp work. They are either laced on the sides or buckled. See GLOVES.

Curlew. A long-billed and long-legged shore bird. In "A Home on the Range," the cowboy sings, "Oh, I love these wild flowers in this dear land of ours; the curlew I love to hear scream." [1]

Cuts. Cattle not suitable for driving up the trail, which are cut out before starting.

[1] From John A. and Alan Lomax, *op. cit.*

Cutting Ground. The spot picked by the range boss where cattle are to be driven during a roundup for cutting out, branding, earmarking, tallying. See ROUNDUP.

Cutting Horse. An especially trained horse used in cutting out cows or calves from a herd. Also called "whittling pony," "whittler," "cut horse," and "peg pony," or "part horse" by Californians. These horses seem to have a superior intelligence which the cowboy calls "cow sense." Once a rider indicates the cow or calf he wants to cut out for branding or some other purpose, the horse is right after the animal, wheeling and turning and worrying it until he gets it away from the herd. Most cutting horses appear to take a delight in their work and are highly prized by their owners. The Quarter Horse is usually considered the best cutting horse. So valuable are these animals that they are seldom used as roping horses or range horses. Cowboys use a deep saddle with long stirrups to keep their seats during the quick, sharp maneuvers of the cutting horse. Cutting-horse contests are very popular in rodeos. See HORSE, QUARTER HORSE, QUICK STOP, RODEO, ROPE HORSE.

Cutting Sign. To find evidence or "sign" that an animal or a man has been in a certain place. A succession of such signs would mean a trail. See RIDING SIGN, SIGN.

Cutting Trail. During a cattle drive a rancher might "cut the trail" of the herd and order the cowboys to stop so he could look for any cattle that might belong to him. This right was given any ranch owner whose range had been crossed by the herd, as his cattle might have joined them.

"Trail cutting" also was a term meaning to cross a trail or to pick up a trail. See CATTLE DRIVE, RIDING SIGN.

Dally. To turn the rope in a counter-clockwise direction several times around the horn of the saddle after throwing it. The term comes from the Mexican *dar la vuelta,* "to give a turn." This was a practice of the California buckaroos, who used a reata, or rawhide rope. The Texan made his hempen rope fast around the saddle horn and was called a "tie-man." But the Californian was known as a "dally-man," and "dallied" his rope because a rawhide rope would not stand the sudden strain when the cow was "busted" on the other end, and dallying allowed it to "give" or slip. This was also called "dally vuelting," "daling," or "vuelting." See HORN, ROPE.

Dam. A female parent horse.

Danglers. Pear-shaped metal ornaments which hang from a cowboy's spurs and jingle when he walks. Also called "jingle-bobs." See SPURS.

Day Herding. The herding of a bunch of cattle cut out from the roundup herd and held apart for shipment to the market. Also, on the trail, the herding of cattle that were held over for a few days' rest and grazing.

Day Wrangler. A cowboy who takes care of the remuda in the daytime. See REMUDA, WRANGLER.

Derringer (dehr'in-jer). A small pistol of large caliber, with two barrels which were parallel or of the over-and-under type. A derringer could be laid in the palm of the hand and carried in the pants pocket. It was .41 caliber and shot a soft-nosed lead bullet which made a terrible wound at a distance of seven to ten feet. It was

the popular gun of the western gambler and later was a "hide-out" gun, used by cowboys when they were forced to check their six-guns with the town marshals. See HIDE-OUT.

Dewlap. The hanging skin under the throat of a cow. This was also a type of brand. See BRANDS.

Die-up. A range-wide destruction of animals from a drought or a snowstorm.

Dofunny. The cowboy's expression for a useless object.

Dog. There were few dogs on the range in the old days. Some Texas ranchers used them to chase "mossy horn" cattle from the chaparral where they hid. Others sometimes used them in packs when wolves became bad. But stray dogs were shot as a menace to cattle. One valuable dog, however, was the "bear dog," usually a small curly little fellow who knew how to keep a grizzly bear at bay by yapping at his heels and making him back up against a tree where he became a good target.

Doggone. A mild slang expression. Whenever he could think of it, this was the word cowboys used around womenfolks.

Dogie (doh'gee). An orphaned calf. In some parts of the West "dogie" meant any young steer. It was usually used affectionately. The term came from the Mexican word *dogal* (doh'gahl), a short rope used to tie a calf while its mother was being milked. In the Southwest the dogie was thought of as a stunted calf "whose mammy is dead and its pappy run off with another cow." One of the many cowboy songs about "little dogies" went, "Git along, git along, git along, little dogies, you're going to be beef steers by-and-by." [1]

Double-Action. A revolver in which the pulling of the trigger automatically cocks the hammer sufficiently to fire it. See PISTOL, SINGLE-ACTION.

Drift. The movement of livestock from one locality to another of their own accord, either to avoid weather conditions or to seek new grazing grounds.

Cross fences, called drift fences, were built to keep cattle from drifting from the home range during blizzards or northers. See BLIZZARD.

Dry Shooting. Sometimes called "dry firing." This was a term for practicing the exact movements of the quick-draw up to the point of aiming, and possibly even pulling the trigger of an empty gun. The cowboy practiced this during his spare moments so he would become expert in the quick-draw. See QUICK-DRAW.

Dude. In the old days, a tenderfoot who came West and tried to be western in dress and manner. Today the meaning has been softened a little to become a "city feller who is a guest on a dude ranch." To show there is no hard feeling, the cowboys allow themselves to be called "roughnecks." A female dude is a "dudeen" or a "dudette."

[1] From John A. and Alan Lomax, *op. cit.*

Dude Horse. A good horse, but gentle-broke and reliable for the use of dudes.

Dude Ranch. The dude ranch of today, as one fellow said, "just growed that way." There are hundreds of them throughout the West and most are working ranches, where stock and cattle are raised as a business, but which take in "paying guests." The ranches vary in size and facilities from a cluster of cabins, offering only horseback riding and hiking, to the elaborate, hotel-like spreads with swimming pools, golf courses, skeet ranges, airfields, and service stations. But they all cater exclusively to that type of American who sees romance in imitating the cowboy's dress and activities.

Dude Wrangler. Boss of a dude ranch.

Duffle Bag. The present-day cowboy's trunk. He sometimes calls it his "hot roll," as the duffle bag, or sack, is his bed. This bed is made up of several comforters, or "sougans," as the cowboys call them (when the roll is being carried in the chuck wagon or bed wagon), and one or two woolen blankets. These are all folded lengthwise and wrapped in a canvas sheet or tarpaulin, which is folded over like an envelope. The cowboy carries most of his belongings in this roll.

Dugout. A one-room dwelling built into the ground or on a hillside. These were popular in the Southwest among the early ranchers, and sometimes a dugout was the first ranch house. They were used, too, by line riders when they built their line camps far from the ranch headquarters. Dugouts also were built by homesteaders and nesters in the cyclone regions, such as Kansas, as a refuge. See Line Rider, Ranch.

Durham. A breed of cattle. The Durham is also called the Shorthorn. These were the first tame cattle brought to the Southwest in the attempt to breed out the long horns of the wild cattle there and to produce a better and more saleable beef animal. The Durham is heavy and stocky, and more noted as a beef animal than as a milch cow. See Cattle.

Dutch Oven. An iron kettle with a flat bottom and heavy iron lid, which rests on three iron legs, used in cow camps for making sour-dough biscuits or "risin' bread."

Hot coals were put underneath and on top of the kettle to bake the dough. See Chuck.

Eagle. A large bird of prey. The so-called Mexican eagle is the golden eagle, or *aquila* (ah-kee'lah), as the Mexicans call it. This bird ranges from the northern Rockies down to central Mexico. The bald eagle, which is our national bird, is also

found as far south as central Mexico. While it is unlawful to kill either bird, cattlemen and sheepmen do hunt them because they carry off calves and lambs. But, for the most part, eagles kill and eat jack rabbits and ground squirrels.

Joe De Yong, the famous cowboy artist, writes, "There is a bit of eagle technique among hunters' lore; which is, when an eagle carries off a lamb or calf it flies very high and drops it among rocks to break all its bones, so it will be easier to tear apart when feeding the young eagles in the nest. Another thing, the old bird teaches the young to fly by carrying them high into the air, dropping them, and then swooping down and catching them before any harm can take place. I have seen this, and while I sympathized with the young one being dropped, what a thrill for the second fledgling, still in the nest, to watch such a performance—knowing its turn came next! Maybe quite a thrill for the little fellow that was being dropped, too!" Today modern ranchers hunt the Mexican eagle from airplanes. They also hunt the big red-tail hawk in the same manner.

Eagle-Bills. Cowboy term for tapaderos with extremely long points which hang well below the stirrups and resemble eagles' beaks. See TAPADEROS.

Ear-Head. A simple headstall, often seen along the Border, with a loop at the top for one or both ears. This type of head-stall has no noseband, browband, or throat-latch, and is used only on horses that have been broken. See HEADSTALL.

Earing Down. Holding a horse's head down by hanging onto his ears while a rider mounts. This practice is commonly used on particularly wild horses. Sometimes the man who is "earing down" will close his teeth over the tip of an ear protruding from the top of his hand. To lead or drive a wild horse easily, his ears are doubled over on themselves and tied tight with horsehair. This seems to stun or stupify the horse and he is easily managed.

Earmark. A method of marking cattle by cutting out certain parts of the ear. In winter, when the cow's hair grew long, it was sometimes hard to see the brand, but earmarks could always be seen. This marking was done with a knife. The expression, "to earmark," comes from this practice and is used today in business when something is labeled for future use. Several types of earmarks are shown below. See BRANDS.

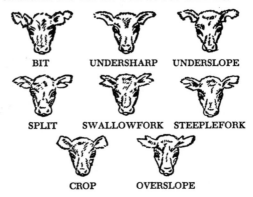

BIT   UNDERSHARP   UNDERSLOPE

SPLIT   SWALLOWFORK   STEEPLEFORK

CROP   OVERSLOPE

Eight-up. A team of eight horses, mules, or oxen.

Enchiladas (en-chee-lah'dahs). A Mexican dish made of corncakes, eggs, and chili peppers. See CHUCK.

Equalizer. Cowboy term for six-gun. It comes from the old western expression that "a Colt makes all men equal." See COLT.

Estrays. Cattle which were recognized during a roundup as belonging on a distant range. These "visitors" were cut out and driven home.

Ewe-Neck. A neck, such as that of some horses, which is thin and bowed backwards, similar to the neck of a ewe or female sheep.

Fall-back. When a horse rears and falls backwards. This is different from the "throw-back," in that the action of falling is not intentional on the part of the horse. The fall-back or back-fall is dangerous for the rider. See THROW-BACK.

Fanning. A term for shooting a single-action or double-action revolver by releasing the trigger and "fanning" the hammer back with the heel of the hand. Usually the trigger and trigger mechanism were removed from the gun. An expert could fire

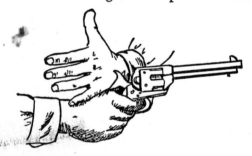

a shot a second by this method. In fanning, the gun was held at hip level with the inner part of the forearm pressed close to the hipbone for support. "Slip shooting" is similar to fanning, only the hammer is thumbed with a wiping motion.

A cowboy also "fanned" a bucking horse by striking him on the neck with his hat. See DOUBLE-ACTION, SINGLE-ACTION.

Fiador (fee'ah-dohr). A safety device or throatlatch on a hackamore. Cowboys commonly call it "Theodore." The fiador is a small doubled rope of either horsehair or sashcord that runs through the loops of the hackamore's brow band at the point just below and behind the ears. Then it goes around the neck, is knotted under the throat, and ends in another and lower knot, so tied that it will not slip over the heel button of the bosal. See BOSAL, HACKAMORE, KNOTS.

Fiador Knot. A difficult knot, rather like the diamond knot in rope work, tied with four strands, two of them closed. See KNOTS.

Filly. A young mare horse. When under one year she is called a "foal." See COLT.

Fish. See SLICKER.

Flanking. A method of throwing a calf by grabbing its flank, over the back and under, and tossing it off balance.

Flapjack. A kind of bread, something like a pancake but larger and made of thicker dough. It is turned over by a quick flip of the frying pan. The flapjack was a very popular item in the cowboy's fare. See CHUCK.

Flier. A printed reward notice for a "bad man" sent out broadcast and tacked on trees and buildings.

Flunky. The driver of the bed wagon at a roundup. See ROUNDUP.

Forging. When a horse's front foot is struck by his back one he is said to be "forging."

Four-Point. A mackinaw with four color lines woven into the edge of the material, which denotes extra quality.

Freighters. Caravans of ox-teams. During the twenty years before the close of the War between the States the freighters moved the Mormon settlers, Oregon emi-grants, western homesteaders, gold seekers, and the Army's supplies across the great plains of the West. See NESTER.

Frijoles (free-ho'lees). A Mexican dried bean used in chili con carne and other Mexican dishes. See CHILI CON CARNE.

Frill. A decoration on a quirt. This is a piece of leather which is cut in little slits and wound around the body of the quirt to form a tassel. See QUIRT.

Frying-Pan Bread. Bread which the old-time cowboy made with flour, water, and baking powder. A thin batter was spread over the bottom of the frying pan, which was placed on the hot coals until a crust formed on the lower part. Then the cowboy tipped the skillet on edge so the heat from the fire could reach the dough and raise the loaf. See CHUCK.

Fuzztails. Sometimes called "fuzzies." These are wild or range horses. See BROOM-TAIL, MUSTANG.

Gait. The manner in which a horse walks or steps.

The slowest gait is the walk. In this movement the horse goes forward always with two or more feet on the ground at the same time.

The second fastest gait is the trot. In trotting a horse lifts a front and hind foot on opposite sides at the same time. The body of the horse is entirely off the ground twice during each stride. The cowboy does not care for this gait, as he "rides close" to the saddle.

Usually the gallop, or "lope" as the cowboy calls it, is considered the third fastest gait in the saddlehorse. However, the cowboy likes to think of it as the second fastest, and the cowboy's horse is trained to break into a lope or gallop from the walk, since the cowboy does not like to ride at a trot. In loping or galloping, the horse may lead with either the right or left foot, but he should always lead with the inside foot on turning. In this gait, the horse appears to take one leap after another. In fact, a gallop is defined as a regular succession of leaps. If while loping the horse suddenly puts only one foot down at a time in short, quick steps, he is said to be "crow hopping."

A canter is a slow gallop. A fast gallop is called "running" by the cowboy, although actually only a two-legged animal can run.

Pacing is the gait of a horse in which both feet on the same side are brought forward at the same time. It is sometimes called the "amble." Racking and single-footing are gaits similar to pacing. However, in racking the motion is quicker and slightly different, called a "quick amble." In single-footing the two legs on the same side are raised almost at the same time, but not simultaneously. The single-footing horse is highly prized by the cowboy and to ride one is "like ridin' in a rocking chair."

Gallop. See GAIT.

Gauge. A unit of measure for a shotgun. The gauge was figured out by taking a lead ball exactly the size of the bore and then finding out how many of these balls could be obtained from a pound of lead. If ten balls could be made from a pound, the gun was 10-gauge; if twelve balls, it was 12-gauge, and so on. See SHOTGUN.

Gear. The cowboy's saddle, bridle, rope,

quirt, and other "tools" of his trade. In recent days among western horsemen, the jockey term "tack" is sometimes used.

Gee! Command to a driven horse, mule, or ox to turn to the right, generally used when driving with a jerkline. See JERKLINE.

Gentle-broke. When a horse has been trained by kindness, he is said to be "gentle-broke." The cowboy makes friends with him, but he never spoils the horse or makes a pet of him. Pet horses are considered the most treacherous, and no cowboy will have anything to do with them. Some Indians gentle-broke their horses, and these were considered valuable saddle horses. See BUST, INDIAN-GENTLED.

Gentling. Another western term for busting or breaking a horse. When the cowboy speaks of "gentling a hoss" he does not mean he will tame it in a gentle fashion, but that he will make it gentle by the time he is through with it. This is not the same as "gentle-broke." See BUST.

Getting the Drop. Beating another man to the draw and covering him. When a gunfighter "got the drop" on his opponent, he did not intend to kill him, but rather to place him at his mercy and take him prisoner or prevent him from using his six-gun. In disarming a man, there were times when cowboys did as they do in the movies today when they say, "Hand me that-'ar gun, butt first." But this went out

of style when one Curly Bill, in handing his gun butt first to the marshal of Tombstone, spun the gun muzzle forward by a quick flip of his wrist, and shot the peace officer. After that gunmen, when captured, were ordered to drop their guns at their feet and step back. See Road Agent's Spin.

Gila Monster (hee'la). A large, poisonous lizard of the Southwest. This reptile is more commonly found in the hot and sandy lowlands along the Gila River, which starts in western New Mexico and crosses Arizona to empty into the Colorado River near Yuma. Gila monsters sometimes grow more than two feet in length and are black and yellow (or orange), with these colors

alternating in rings on the tail. Small animals are killed or paralyzed by their bite, which also produces severe symptoms in humans.

Girth. Texas term for cincha. See Cincha.

Git! One of the most forceful words of the old West. When a man said "Git!" or "Now you git!" it meant "Go" or the next word might be spoken by his six-gun.

Glass Eye. See Pinto.

Gloves. In cold weather all cowboys wear gloves. In warm weather most of them wear gloves when roping or riding bucking broncos. But some old-time cow-

boys wore gloves all the time, and this was to show the other cowboys that they were

so good at riding and roping they did not have to do any other kind of work. The hands of these experts were soft and white as those of a girl.

Gloves are made of horsehide or buckskin, mostly brown, but some are yellow, gray, or a greenish or creamy white. In the early days, most gloves had gauntlets or cuffs which were decorated with stitching of silk thread or small silver or brass wire. The Lone Star design was popular. Many gloves formerly had buckskin fringe along the little finger side, but this has now gone out of fashion. The modern cowboy is more likely to wear a short glove and separate leather cuff. See Cuff.

Go-Devil. A device for getting water out of a stream with high banks. A wire led down from the bank and was anchored in the stream. On the wire was a bucket with a rope attached which could be sent down empty and pulled back full.

Good Mouthed. When a horse responds quickly to the slightest pressure on the bit, he is said to be "good mouthed." The opposite is "hard mouthed."

Granger. A farmer. It is from the word Grange, which in the East meant a local branch of the Order of Patrons of Husbandry. The farmer also was called by the cowboy a "fool hoe-man." The cowboy resented the coming of the farmer to the open range as he settled near watering places and fenced them in. See NESTER.

Grass. There were numerous types of grass on the open range of the old West, most of them grouped under the common name of "bunch grass." These included mesquite grass and grama grass, the latter sometimes called "dog's grass." Bunch grasses were found on the prairies and in regions where there was little rain. Buffalo grass, common to the higher regions, particularly the Staked Plains, was a mosslike grass and especially good as fodder in winter. In the northern sections a grass known as "blue joint" was common. It grew knee-high to a cow and matured into a very nourishing head, like wheat or rye. In marshy regions tall, luxuriant grasses grew, but cattle rarely grazed upon them as they were the home of noxious insects. See OPEN RANGE, STAKED PLAINS.

Greaser. Western term for a Mexican.

Greenhorn. Anyone new to a business. Evidently from the sprouting new horns of a young calf.

Gringo (gring'go). The Mexican name for foreigners and especially for Americans across the Border. It is not, as some think, a Mexican word, but is used throughout Spanish-speaking countries to mean a "foreigner." It is from the Spanish slang word for *griego*, meaning Greek. To *hablar en gringo*, or "speak in Greek," is slang for speaking in a language that cannot be understood, as we say, "It's Greek to me."

Grip. The "grip" was very important to the old-time gun-toter. It was the one spot in his gun hand between the last joints of

the thumb and forefinger where the stock of the gun rested to enable him to have one straight line from muzzle to elbow. He practiced holding his gun in that position until it became second nature to him and he could point his weapon just like he

pointed his finger. The grip was very important in the quick-draw and hip-firing. See HIP-FIRING, QUICK-DRAW.

Gun. This was the term the old-time cowboy commonly used for his pistol or revolver. He rarely called a rifle or carbine a "gun," except possibly in the case of buffalo gun. A shotgun was an exception, and was often referred to as a "scatter gun."

Today the term "gun" is applied correctly only to a sporting arm of smooth bore, such as a shotgun. See BUFFALO GUN, COLT, PISTOL, SHOTGUN, WINCHESTER.

Gunfighter. A term usually applied to men who were experts in the use of the six-gun, but who were on the side of the law. A marshal or a Ranger might be known as a "gunfighter," but an outlaw like Billy the Kid would be a "gunman." See TOWN MARSHAL.

Gunman. A gunman was not only a man who carried a six-gun, but one who knew how to use it. "Gunman" was a term applied generally to outlaws, "long riders," and cattle rustlers who were quick to shoot. Law enforcement officers preferred to be known as "gunfighters." See BAD MAN, LONG RIDER, RUSTLER.

Hackamore. A type of western bridle without a bit. The word is from the Mexican *jáquima* (hah'key-mah). The hackamore consists of a headstall, a bosal, a mecate (may-kah'tay), and a fiador (fee'ahdohr). The bosal fits around the nose of

the horse and is attached to the headstall. The mecate is a hair rope which is used as reins and lead rope. The fiador is a safety device similar to the throatlatch on an ordinary bridle.

The hackamore has been very popular in the West, and particularly in California, for breaking horses. It is considered by many cowboys as the best instrument to teach a horse to neck rein. Later, when the horse has been broken, a bridle with bit is used. See BIT, BOSAL, FIADOR, KNOTS, MECATE.

Hair Trigger. A trigger on a gun or rifle adjusted for a very light pull. By filing the notch on the hammer the cowboy could make his gun a hair-trigger weapon so that it went off at a mere touch of his trigger finger. See PISTOL.

Hamstringing. Cutting the large sinew of an animal's hind leg just above the hock. Wolves often would hamstring a cow or horse, thus crippling it, and making it easier to kill. See WOLF.

Hand. The unit of measurement for a horse's height. Four inches make a hand. A horse is said to be so many "hands" high, measuring at the shoulder level. See HORSE.

Handle. Name. A "handle" might be a man's full name or merely his nickname. It did not matter to cowboys, just so they had something to call a man by. It was impolite in the West to ask a man his full name or inquire into his background. So cowboys merely asked, "What's your handle?" See NICKNAMES.

Hangout. A meeting place for rustlers and outlaws. It was also called "hide-out." Some of the famous hangouts were the Robbers' Roost in Utah, haunt of the "Wild Bunch"; Castle Rock in the Henry Mountains, where the "Blue Mountain Gang" holed up; the Hole in the Wall, favorite hiding place of the "Hole in the Wall Gang"; Brown's Park County in Colorado; and No Man's Land in the Indian Territory, now Oklahoma. See BAD MAN, NO MAN'S LAND.

Hard Case. A tough hombre or bad man. See BAD MAN.

Hardware. This might mean a cowboy's gun. But it usually means the metal pots, pans, cups, and other kitchen utensils carried in the chuck wagon. See CHUCK WAGON.

Hat. The hat is one of the most important parts of a cowboy's dress. While he wants the very best and sometimes decorates his hat, it is, like his boots, built for both beauty and use. The wide brim is a sunshade, and the high crown is just as important for coolness as is the attic in a house. The cowboy uses his hat to fan a campfire into life; to carry water for his horse, filling the crown; as a pillow on the hard ground; as a drinking cup by holding the brim between his thumb and fingers and forming a trough; for "fanning" a bucking bronco by slapping him on the neck; for signaling, and for many other purposes.

Buying a hat was a long-time investment to the old-time cowboy, who would pay from two to six months' wages for one. Some felts were so soft they could be folded up like handkerchiefs. Like good leather, the fine felt of the cowboy's hat improved with age and hard wear. In time it became a part of him and assumed a shape all its own.

The hat remained on the cowboy's head nearly all the time. He sat down to the table with it on and wore it when he danced with his girl. He touched the brim with his right hand or even took it off with a sweep when he met anyone. This took his right hand away from the vicinity of his gun and showed he was friendly. He thought it unlucky to put his hat on a bunk or bed and usually "hung" it on the floor.

The typical hat of the old-time cowboy was soft, smooth felt, commonly of a dove-gray, but sometimes a light brown or even black. The crown was about seven inches high. Cowboys in different sections dented the crown in different ways, and one could tell where a cowboy came from by the way he creased his hat. In the Southwest the crown was left high, with three or four dents in its sides. In the Northwest the crown was flat on top, but telescoped with a pleat in it which made it lower. Later,

Northwesterners began wearing the peaked hat of the Southwest, and the War Department has called this type of hat the "Montana peak," forgetting that it was originally the "Texas peak."

The first thing a cowboy does on buying a new hat is to place it in water, being sure none gets inside the crown, and then creasing it to suit himself. Around the lower part of the crown, after removing the silk tape there, he places his own type of hatband, which may be woven horsehair, a carved and stamped strap with buckle, or a snake skin. The hat band serves as decoration and also to tighten or loosen the hat to fit the wearer's head. Some hats have "bonnet strings," which come down from beneath the brim and in back of the head to hold the hat on in windy weather. If the brim of an old hat becomes too floppy, slits are made around the edge of the brim and a thong of buckskin or soft leather is woven in. See STETSON.

Haw!　Command to a driven horse, mule, or ox to turn left. See JERKLINE.

Hazing.　Herding or driving. In the old West it might also mean making a tenderfoot dance by shooting near his feet.

Hazing Horse.　A horse which is ridden alongside or near an unruly bronc to quiet him down. In rodeo bulldogging, the term is also used for the horse ridden alongside the bull. See BUST, RODEO.

Headstall.　More often called simply "head" or "bridle head." This is the part of the bridle which fits over the horse's head. It is composed of cheek pieces, crownpiece, noseband, browband, nosepiece, and throatlatch. The bit is attached to the headstall by hooks or buckles. Formerly, some headstalls were simply long straps with

buckles on each end for the bit. This type of headstall was kept on the horse's head by a loop or loops (or perhaps a slit in

the strap) which passed over the horse's ear or ears. Fancy headstalls are made from braided rawhide, horsehair, and leather. Some expensive ones are made from woven silver wire. They are decorated with silver conchas and other ornaments. See BIT, BRIDLE, LEATHER BRAIDING.

Heifer Brand.　The "brand" put on cowboys at a dance where there was a shortage of female partners for the square dance. Certain cowboys took the place of the womenfolks, and their "brand" was a neckerchief tied around the arm.

Herd.　The cowboy spoke of a "herd" of cattle and a "band" of horses. He might call both a "bunch." When a herd of cattle was made up entirely of steers, cowboys called it a "beef herd." If it was mixed with cows, it was a "cow herd," as cowboys liked to use the word "cow" wherever possible. See BAND.

Hereford.　A breed of cattle, usually red with white markings or spots. The Hereford is a short-legged breed and is considered the best type of domesticated cattle adapted to the range. See CATTLE.

Hickok, James Butler (Wild Bill). One of the greatest gunfighters of the West, called by Emerson Hough "The beau ideal of the Western Bad Men." He was not a "bad man" in the sense of being an outlaw or desperado but in that he was what the West called "a bad man to trifle with."

Hickok was born on May 27, 1837, in La Salle County, Illinois. He went west at the age of eighteen and saw fighting during the guerrilla days in Kansas before the War between the States. Later, after working as a stage driver for the Overland Stage Line, he was stationed at Rock Creek Station in Jefferson County, Nebraska, to guard the company's horses. While there, on December 16, 1861, he killed David McCanles and two companions, after McCanles, who was having trouble with the stage line over the sale of some property, went to the station with the purpose of "cleaning it up."

Hickok served during the War between the States with the Union forces as a scout and sharpshooter. His reputation as a gunfighter grew, and he was no doubt given more credit for successful gunplay than he deserved. But he was feared and respected as a "quick-draw" man and a killer. It was

said that even though another man had the drop on him he could whip out his six-gun and, firing from the hip, kill the other before he could pull the trigger of his own gun. Also that he could shoot from the hip and hit two cans, one on either side of the road, by firing both his guns at once. He was a master of the "grip."

There were a lot of wild stories about Wild Bill. When the cow towns began to roar at the railroad terminals in Kansas in the 1860's and 1870's, Wild Bill became marshal first at Hays City and later at Abilene. He killed several desperadoes during this time. He wore his hair long and carried his six-guns in the waistband of his trousers, butts pointing inwards for a double cross draw. He also carried the wicked little .41 caliber derringer pistol and killed a well-known gambler with this gun. Wild Bill was said to have always made it a rule to give his victims funerals.

When Ned Buntline opened a western theatrical thriller on the Bowery, Wild Bill joined the company with Buffalo Bill Cody, his friend. But Wild Bill left in disgust because of objections to his firing his blank cartridges too close to the moccasins of the dancing Indians in the show.

Wild Bill was killed on August 2, 1876, at Deadwood, South Dakota, by Jack McCall, who wanted to "gain a reputation" by killing the famous gunfighter. He walked behind Wild Bill as the latter was sitting at a card table and shot him in the back of the head. Although Wild Bill was killed "instantly," so quick were his reactions that it was said he had drawn his six-gun part way from the holster before he fell to the floor. He was thirty-nine when he died, and although some said he had killed two men for every year of his life, this was certainly not true. But his accuracy with the six-gun has never been disputed. See Cross Draw, Grip, Hip-firing, Town Marshal.

Hide-out. A term used for a gun that is concealed. The hide-out became popular when gun-toting was prohibited in the wild and woolly cow towns. The cowboy would check his regular gun and holster with the town marshal, but would have another one

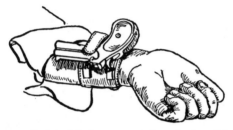

concealed in his boot, waistband, shoulder holster, or perhaps hung by a cord down his coat or shirt sleeve. When the small .41 caliber derringer came into use, it was termed a "hide-out gun." See Derringer, Sleeve Draw.

Hip-firing. Firing a pistol from the hip without sighting it. This was the trick of the "quick-draw man," of which one of the best was Wild Bill Hickok, who could fire effectively two guns from the hip at the same time. In hip-firing, the gun was held at the level of the hip with the forearm pressed close to the hipbone for support. The gun was usually discharged by fanning. To fire from the hip, or the minute the gun was drawn from the holster, the

cowboy had to grip the gun in such a manner that pointing it was like pointing his finger. To master this grip he had to practice long and hard. Sometimes the gun was

not removed from the holster but was fired right through the open toe. This type of holster was on a swivel. See Fanning, Grip, Hickok, Holster.

Hitching. Tying a horse. Most horses used by cowboys were so well trained that the minute the reins were dropped to the ground they would stand still. The reins were split on the ends and the cowboy just let them go when he dismounted. If the horse started to walk, he stepped on the reins and the bit would cut his mouth. But some horses had to be hitched, and if there was a convenient post or fence a cowboy usually hitched his horse anyway. He might just wrap the reins around several times, but usually he tied them to the post or fence.

There were several methods of tying a horse. When the cowboy was on the plains and there was nothing to which he could hitch his horse, he might dig a hole in the ground, tie the reins around a bone or stick, and thrust this into the hole. The anchor would not come up unless pulled directly upwards. The cowboy could even hitch his horse to some bunch grass if necessary when he was in open country.

Hobbles. Cuffs or loops of leather or other material which are fastened around a horse's forefeet just above the pastern joint and connected with a short chain or thong. Hobbled horses can move their feet only a few inches and therefore cannot wander far, although some horses learn to jump with both forefeet together and manage to get miles away during the night.

Hobbles are of various types. The majority are straps of cowhide or buckskin made into cuffs or loops at both ends and twisted in the center. The cuffs are fastened with leather buttons or buckles. Other types of hobbles are made from rope and a torn gunnysack tied in knots to produce

loops. The overall length of the average hobble is thirteen and one-half inches. See CROSS HOBBLE, SIDE-LINING.

Hoecake. This is a corn bread made of corn meal, bacon grease, hot water, and salt. In the "Cowboy's Gettin'-Up Holler," the song goes, "Wake up, Jacob, day's a-breakin'; Fryin' pan's on an' hoecake's bakin'."[1] The meal, salt, and bacon fat are first put in a container and scalding water poured over them. The mixture is thoroughly stirred to form a batter not too stiff and not too thin, then allowed to remain a while so the meal can swell. It is placed in a hot, well-greased frying pan, cooked on one side, flipped over, and cooked on the other. There is nothing more delicious. The name "hoecake" came from the custom in the South of cooking the bread on a hot hoe. See CHUCK.

[1] From John A. and Alan Lomax, *op. cit.*

Hogback. Term for tops of small hills that lead back into the mountain divide. Also a term for a horse with a roached back.

Hog-Leg. A six-shooter. Sometimes it was pronounced "hawg-leg" and other times "hawg's leg." The butt of the old Colt six-gun was shaped like a hog's leg.

Hog-tie. To fasten the two hind legs and one front leg of an animal together. Sometimes pronounced "hawg-tie." The cowboy uses a "piggin' string" to hog-tie a calf.

Hole Up. To hide out, as rustlers and outlaws did when the law was after them.

Hollow Horn. A "disease" that puzzled the tenderfoot. Cows' horns dropped off after a freeze. As they were, of course, hollow, the tenderfoots were told that the cows suffered from "hollow horn."

Holster. A leather sheath in which the six-gun is carried. The old-time cowboy's holster, by its form and the position in which it was carried on the hip, was designed for the quick-draw. There was no flap to interfere with the rapid withdrawal of the gun. The holster was hung from a loose-fitting belt and was just far enough down so that the arm was slightly curved when the hand grasped the butt of the gun. If the holster was too high the gun might jam; if too low the cowboy could not get it quickly. A split second's delay in withdrawing the gun might mean death. When riding, the holster was hung on the left side so the butt of the gun was forward and the cowboy used the cross draw.

There was a "buscadero" holster which hung from the belt in a slanting position so the barrel of the gun inclined to the rear and the butt was slightly forward, which made for a quicker draw. There were "open-toed" holsters through which the gun could be pointed and fired without drawing it. Such a holster was usually a "swivel holster" and was hung from the belt with a string or a metal swivel. The "half-breed

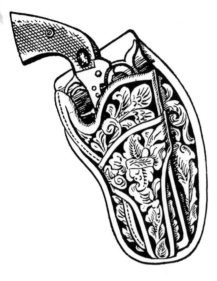

spring holster" was a regular holster but with an open side. The spring which held the gun in position was covered by the holster front. This type of holster was worn as a shoulder holster. The shoulder holster was strapped around the chest so the holster rested under the arm. This was usually a "hide-out," for when a coat was worn the gun and holster were concealed. The shoulder holster is said to have been invented by Ben Thompson, ex-Confederate soldier and gambler.

Holsters were commonly decorated with carved or stamp work and some had thongs at the toe of the holster which could be tied around the lower part of the leg. See BELT, CROSS DRAW, HIDE-OUT, PISTOL, QUICK-DRAW.

Holster Vest. A skeleton vest of soft calfskin with two holster pockets slanting outward from the hip bones. The guns were carried with the butts forward for the cross-arm draw. This vest is credited to John Wesley Hardin, notorious southwestern outlaw. See HOLSTER.

Holt. When a cowboy fastened onto anything, he got a good "holt." He spoke of an "ear holt," "tail holt," or "head holt."

Hombre (ohm'bray). Spanish for "man." A favorite word in the West and Southwest. Cowboys spoke of "good hombres" and "bad hombres," pronouncing the word "umbry." In Mexico a champion, or he-man, is *hombre de hombre.*

Honda (hon'da). The eye on the working end of the lariat through which the rope passes to form the loop or noose. It is derived from the Spanish *honda* (ohn-dah) meaning "sling" or "slingshot." The simplest form of honda for a manila or maguey rope is made with the "honda

knot." An overhand knot is tied a short distance from the end of the rope and the end is then passed through the knot. Another overhand knot is made in the very end and both honda knot and overhand knot are jammed together, as shown in the illustration. The finished eye should be about two inches long. Sometimes a piece of leather called a "wear leather" is placed over the end of the eye to protect it. The honda also can be formed by splicing an eye into the rope, but usually this splice is made around a "thimble" or metal honda.

In rawhide ropes, or reatas, the honda is made with a thick piece of rawhide, about three-quarters of an inch wide. This is rolled into a circle two inches in diameter with the ends overlapping. Through these ends a hole is made and the end of the reata passed through and secured with a knot on the inside. An eye splice also can be made and the eye covered with leather. See BITTER END, KNOTS, ROPE.

Hoodoo. See RUSTLER.

Hooking Up. A term meaning the harnessing of work horses.

Hoop Snake. According to cowboy legend, a snake that catches his tail in his mouth and rolls along like a hoop. Usually a reptile that tenderfoots were told to look out for, as a joke.

Hoosegow. A cowboy word for jail. It came from his pronunciation of the Spanish *juzgado* (hooth-gah'do), meaning court or tribunal. See CALABOOSE.

Horn. The pommel or knob on the front of a saddle. Saddle horns vary in height and shape depending upon whether they are used for securing the rawhide rope or the hard-twist rope. The horn of the Mexican saddle is the shape of an orange cut in half with the flat part uppermost, while the

cowboy's saddle horn is higher with a smaller knob. Some horns are covered with wrapped or braided rawhide. See DALLY, SADDLE, TIE-MAN.

Horned Toad. A species of Mexican lizard found in the Southwest. They have spikes on their heads and spiny scales down

their backs which protect them from being swallowed by snakes. They live on insects, bask in the sun, and can run very fast. It is said they can live years without food.

Horse. The cowboy's horse came from the Mexican horse. The Mexicans, or Spanish Indians, had got their horses from the Spanish invaders. And Spaniards rode the horse which the Moors had introduced into Spain around the eighth century.

Once there had been horses on the American continent, as shown by fossil remains which have been found in Wyoming, but they disappeared about the time of the Ice Age. Thus horses came back to America after thousands of years when Cortes, Narvaez, and other Spanish conquerers brought them into Mexico beginning around 1519.

The Mexican Indians were terrorized at first by the sight of the horse, but later they used this animal as they did the firearms the Spaniards brought. Horses began to multiply and bands of them became wild and roamed across the Rio Grande, traveling as far north as the present-day boundary of Canada. The Plains Indians captured these horses and were then able to ride the Great Plains and hunt the buffalo. The horse did as much for the Indians as the railroad later did for the white man.

It has been said the cowboy got his horse from the Indian pony. This is only partly

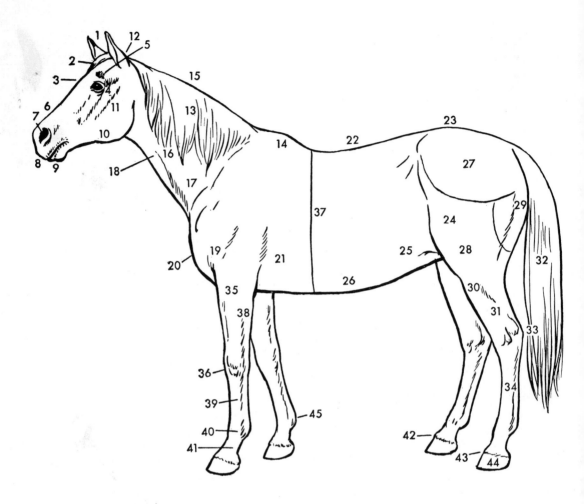

1. EARS	16. THROAT	31. LEG
2. FORELOCK	17. NECK	32. TAIL
3. FOREHEAD	18. JUGULAR VEIN	33. HOCK
4. EYE	19. SHOULDER	34. CANNON
5. EYEPITS	20. BREAST	35. FORELEG
6. NOSE	21. RIBS	36. KNEE
7. NOSTRIL	22. BACK	37. GIRTH
8. MUZZLE	23. LOINS	38. ELBOW
9. LIPS	24. HIP	39. SHANK
10. JAW	25. FLANK	40. FETLOCK JOINT
11. CHEEK	26. BELLY	41. PASTERN
12. POLL	27. HAUNCH	42. CORONET
13. MANE	28. THIGH	43. FOOT
14. WITHERS	29. BUTTOCK	44. HOOF
15. CREST	30. STIFLE	45. FETLOCK

true. He captured and tamed wild horses just as the Indians did. The wild horse was ideal for the cowboy's use. He had speed and endurance and was easy to manage when tamed. But he was a small horse, weighing around 600 pounds. Later ranchmen improved the cow horse by breeding him with imported stock from the East. This new type of horse was both larger, weighing about 800 pounds, and of a more gentle nature.

The cowboy prized a good saddle horse. The Texas Rangers had a saying which applied to the cowboy, too: "A Ranger is no better than his horse." Cowboys, who paid forty dollars for a saddle and ten dollars for a horse (if they bought him instead of catching him), still appreciated his worth, and the saying was, "You ride the horse and not the saddle." See APPALOOSA, ARABIAN, CAYUSE, CUTTING HORSE, MORGAN, MUSTANG, PALOMINO, PINTO, QUARTER HORSE, ROPE HORSE, STOCK HORSE, THOROUGHBRED.

Horseback Opinion. A term in the Southwest meaning gossip. News and gossip spread with great rapidity through the cow country. Riders would always stop upon meeting and exchange the latest facts.

Horsehair Rope. Ropes braided from horsehair were much used by early cowboys. They are as old as the horse in the American West, for Indians and Mexicans employed these ropes for centuries. The Mexican called them *mecates*, which the cowboy promptly rechristened "McCartys." The mecate is important on the hackamore and is still used.

Formerly the horsehair rope was used as a "throw rope" or "catch rope," but because of its roughness and lightness and tendency to kink, it gave way to the "hard twist" ropes of hemp and maguey. However, a cowboy usually carried a short horsehair rope tied to his saddle, even if only as a protection against rattlesnakes, tarantulas, and centipedes, which would not cross a horsehair rope. It was laid in a circle, inside of which the cowboy slept. But the horsehair rope did not always work with rattlesnakes, and a cowboy sleeping in a horsehair rope circle might awake in the morning with a rattler curled up on his chest. When rattlers are shedding they are blind and will crawl over anything.

Mexican and Indian-made horsehair ropes are still made and are sold by western cowboy and saddlery outfitters. The best quality is the "clipped" rope made from the horse's mane. See HACKAMORE, MECATE, RATTLESNAKE, TARRABEE.

Horse Pullers. Cowboys who traveled with livestock on train journeys. Also called "bull nurses."

Horse Stealing. This was one of the worst crimes of the old West. The cattle thief might get off easy in comparison with the horse thief. If not hanged, the thief was banished after the top of his ear had been cut off. For this reason cowboys distrusted men with long hair, thinking they were covering up a cropped ear. The main reason horse stealing was considered such a major crime was because there were few things more terrible for a cowboy than to be left without his horse miles from water or a ranch. Every time a horse was stolen the cowboy could see himself in such a helpless condition. See LONG HAIR, LYNCHING, RUSTLER.

Horse Talk. A kind of talk used by Indians when working with horses. The cowboy got his "whoa" from the "hoh, hoh," of the Indians, who believed this was "talk" that the horse could understand. Indian horse talk was a low grunt, which was uttered deep in the chest and sounded like "hoh, hoh." Indians claimed this charmed a horse and made him stand still for a moment to listen. See INDIAN-GENTLED.

Horse Thief. See HORSE STEALING.

Horse Wrangler. A man who takes care of saddle horses. See WRANGLER.

Hoss. Cowboy lingo for horse.

Hot Roll. Bedding carried in the bed wagon during a roundup. See DUFFLE BAG.

How! Indian for "howdy." The Plains Indians learned this from the cowboys, as they had no word for greeting. Instead, when one Indian met another he would say, "Fill up the pipe; let us smoke." To express "How!" in the Indian sign language, the Indian bowed his head and body, held his right hand, back to the right, in front of his breast, height of the shoulder, index finger pointing upward, and other fingers closed and with thumb resting on the second finger. He then moved the hand slightly to the left and a little downward, at the same time closing the index finger over the thumb.

This also was the Indian's way of saying "yes." See INDIAN SIGN LANGUAGE.

Huahy! Huahy! (hoo-ay'). What the cowboy shouted when he was driving cattle.

Hull. Cowboy term for saddle.

Hung Up. When a cowboy's foot is caught in a stirrup or he is entangled in some way and dragged while riding a runaway bronc, he is "hung up." See BOOT.

Hurrahing. A cowboy term for his "good-by" to a town, after he had been on a spree. The cowboy came in, spent all his money or lost it gambling, and then gave the town "the rolls" as he rode out at breakneck speed on his horse, shooting his six-gun and yelling like an Indian. This he called "hurrahing" a town.

Hurrah Towns. Term used for old cow towns where the cowboy had fun or a "hurrah time." See COW TOWNS.

Indian. The cowboy put all Indians in two classes—"bad Injuns" and "good Injuns." The worst, in his opinion, were the Comanches and Apaches. He respected the Sioux, Cheyenne, and Arapahoes, who were great fighters and brave men. Such Indians as the Apaches, Lipans, Comanches, and Kickapoos he called "hoss Injuns."

The cowboy began to have his greatest troubles with the Indians as the buffalo disappeared from the plains. The Indians then raided the cow herds to obtain food. The cowboy was always alert on nights when the moon was full, as this was the favorite time for Indians to make their raids. The Indians also held up stagecoaches, swept down on lonely ranches, and stampeded bands of horses. These raids usually were for the purpose of getting a supply of guns and horses.

When the railroads pushed through Kansas, Nebraska, and Wyoming, the Indians gradually became less troublesome. The Army was sweeping the red man into reservations. But Indians were hostile until 1876, and even after that they occasionally broke bounds and went on the warpath. Cowboys would find a ranch house smoldering and the occupants dead or missing.

Sometimes cowboys went with soldiers to help put down Indian uprisings. As the cattle herds going up the Texas Trail passed through the Indian Territory, some Indian tribes asked as high as ten cents a head and others demanded cows for food as tribute for crossing their territory.

The "hoss Injuns" were fine horsemen. They rode with a light pad saddle and could use a speeding pony as a shield, hanging onto its side and shooting from beneath its neck. They always mounted a horse from the right, or off side—the opposite from the cowboy. Some "Injun-gentled" ponies were considered valuable as saddle horses, as they had been broken by kindness. Sometimes, however, the Indian was as cruel as any man could be in "busting" his mount.

The cowboy had to know Indians, and in some instances be familiar with the Indian sign language in order to communicate with them. He adopted the Indian methods of following trails or "riding sign." He used the Indian wickey-up, both as a steam bath and as a temporary shelter, and Indian-tanned buckskin was considered valuable for shirts and vests. Navajo saddle blankets were the best blankets. The cowboy used the Indian war whoop when he treated a cow town to the "rolls," yelling and firing off his six-gun as he rode away. See APACHE, ARAPAHO, ARROW, BOW, BUCKSKIN, BUFFALO, CHEYENNE, COMANCHE, HOW, INDIAN SIGN LANGUAGE, INDIAN-GENTLED, PAD SADDLE, RIDING SIGN, SCALP, SQUAW MAN, WICKEY-UP.

Indian-gentled. An "Injun-gentled" horse was highly valued by the cowboy. After an Indian had roped his unbroken horse he would put a halter on him, approaching him gently and trying to show the horse that he was not going to be hurt. He would keep talking Indian "horse talk." The Indian would spend days with the horse. He would frighten him by hissing and waving a blanket in his face. Then he

would try to show that none of these things hurt. He would patiently touch every part of the horse, and never try to ride him before he could do this successfully. Finally, he would lay his arms across the horse's back and pull himself up a little more each day. When he felt the horse was "gentled," he got on him and the horse would trot off without bucking. See BUST, INDIAN, HORSE.

Indian Sign Language. A system of signs, much like that of deaf-mutes, by which various Indian tribes talked with one another. The cowboy had to know at least enough of the Indian sign language

to be able to tell whether a band of Indians was friendly or hostile.

The sign language is believed to have started back in the days when the Indians first came to the plains to hunt buffalo. They had to have some way of telling whether other Indians they met were friends or enemies. As no two tribes spoke the same language, they developed the sign language to the point where it was almost as perfect as speech.

The Indian sign language was divided into two types. There were the natural signs, like flapping the arms up and down to mean a bird. The other kind called for signs which had to be made up by agreement to mean the names of tribes or persons. Indians were too proud or too lazy to try to understand the spoken language of another tribe. Even the Arapahoes and Cheyenne, who lived together and married into each other's tribes, had to communicate by signs. See HOW, SIGNALS.

Inside Circle. The cutting grounds at a roundup, where cattle to be branded were cut from the herd. This was inside the large circle which comprised all the cattle gathered in the roundup. See ROUNDUP.

Jack Rabbit. A rabbit of the western plains with very long ears, which can run very fast. When a cowboy wanted to shoot a jack rabbit he whistled, and the rabbit would stop and sit up on its haunches. These rabbits are too tough for eating.

Java. Cowboy lingo for coffee. See CHUCK.

Jawbone. Cowboy lingo for credit. When a cowboy said he "called his jaw-bone," he meant that he lived on credit.

Jerked Meat (Jerkie). A dried meat prepared by Plains Indians. The meat was either jerked off the carcass or cut in thin strips and the strips placed on horizontal poles and dried in the sun. Three days of sunny weather were sufficient to cure the meat. It was usually eaten without being cooked. Mexicans called this *charqui* (tchar'kee). When pounded and stored in bags it was known as "pemmican." See PEMMICAN.

Jerkline. A line, or rein, which was attached to the bit of the leader of a string of horses, mules, or oxen harnessed to a wagon. When the driver gave a steady single pull to the line the animal turned to the left; two or more sharp jerks turned him to the right. The driver might also shout "Haw!" when he gave the single pull, and "Gee!" when he gave the two jerks.

Jerky. Slang name for stagecoach. See STAGECOACH.

Jingle-Bobs. See DANGLERS, SPURS.

Jorongo (ho-rohn'go). The Mexican poncho. See PONCHO, SARAPE, SLICKER.

Kack. Cowboy slang for an ordinary saddle. He might say his saddle was just a "Texas kack."

Kettle. To buck or pitch. See BUCKING.

Killer. A very vicious and dangerous horse which tries to unseat his rider by rearing and throwing himself backward. See OUTLAW, THROW-BACK.

King Snake. A large snake of a black and brilliant yellow or orange coloring,

harmless to humans but the deadly enemy of the rattlesnake. A king snake was often kept in a ranch house where there might

be rattlers around. When a rattlesnake ventured in, the king snake streaked after him, twisted himself around the rattler, sunk his fangs just below the rattler's jaw, and squeezed him to death. He never ate his victim. Cowboys arranged fights between king snakes and rattlesnakes, but there was no betting unless a tenderfoot was around. The king snake always won.

Kitchen Gear. Pots, pans, and other cooking utensils carried in the chuck wagon. See CHUCK WAGON, HARDWARE.

Knife Fighting. Fighting with the long knife was looked down upon by the cowboy. He considered it a "greaser's way of fighting." He put his reliance in his six-gun. Not that he was afraid of a knife, but the gun was the quicker way to settle an argument. A knife fight might last as long as half an hour with both fighters cut and slashed and bleeding. Standing foot to foot, with poncho draped over the left arm as a shield, fighters could do a lot of damage to each other. But it was astonishing how many cuts a man might receive and still keep fighting.

Knife fighting was an art, much like boxing. Knife fighters tried all kinds of tricks to throw each other off guard. Sometimes a knife fighter would back up, trailing his poncho on the ground. If the other stepped on it he jerked it and threw his opponent off balance.

A cowboy is quoted as saying, "A knife is a plumb ungentlemanly weepon, and it shore leaves a mussy corpse." The cowboy discarded the long knife after the Indian troubles were over, and rarely carried one unless hunting or in "greaser territory." The knife, as the Latin-Americans say, "is used to open an animal or close a conversation." See BOWIE KNIFE, KNIFE THROWING.

Knife Throwing. At a distance of about thirty feet the long knife, thrown by an expert, was considered the deadliest weap-on of the old West. A knife-thrower could pull his knife and send it to the mark before a man could draw his six-gun and fire it.

The knife was held in the open palm of the hand, never by the blade. It was held in position by a slight pressure of the thumb. The arm was brought back just over the shoulder and the knife hurled by a quick forward and downward motion. If, when the arm was over the shoulder, the blade of the knife was pointing to the rear, it was thrown so that it made only a half turn in the air. This was effective for short distances. If the point was forward, the knife turned one and one half times. A throw of this type was effective for fifty feet or more. To be a good knife thrower required considerable practice. See BOWIE KNIFE, KNIFE FIGHTING.

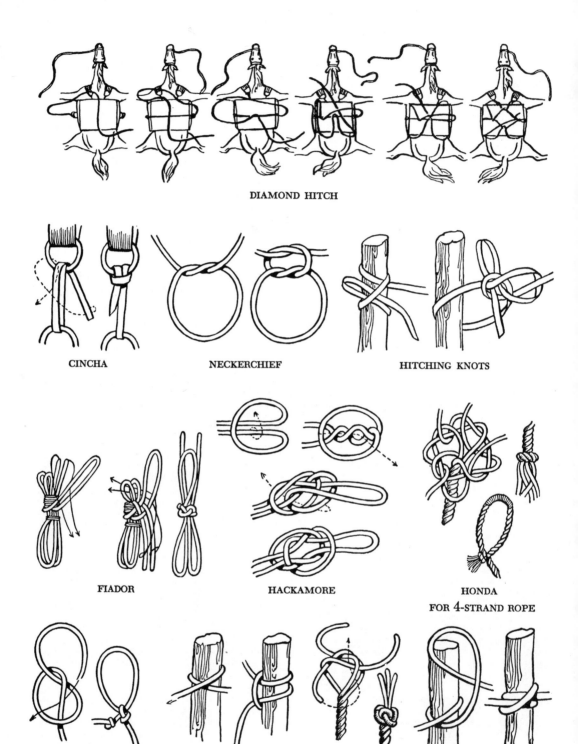

DIAMOND HITCH

CINCHA   NECKERCHIEF   HITCHING KNOTS

FIADOR   HACKAMORE   HONDA

FOR 4-STRAND ROPE

HONDA   HALF HITCH   COW HITCH   BITTER END   CLOVE HITCH

Knots. Intertwinings of one or more parts of rope, cord, leather, or rawhide so they will not slip or come unfastened. The cowboy uses several varieties of knots for tying up horses or cows, for securing loads on pack saddles, and in connection with his gear. During his spare time a cowboy will practice tying knots. Some are more expert than others and keep their methods of tying the harder knots a secret, charging other cowboys for making them. For instance, a cowboy who knew how to tie a fiador knot, one of the hardest of all knots, would charge from fifty to seventy-five cents for each knot he tied.

A few of the more important knots are described below.

BITTER END KNOT. This is the knot for fastening off the end of a rope so it will not unravel. It is known as a "terminal Turk's head knot." The rope also can be finished off with a back splice, where the strands are spliced back into the rope.

CINCHA KNOT. This is the knot used to tie the latigo on the cincha ring. It is sometimes called a "necktie knot" and in sailor's language is known as the "buntline hitch."

CLOVE HITCH. This is a double half hitch in which both half hitches are made in the same direction. It is good for fastening the end of a rope to a post.

COW HITCH. This also is a double half hitch, but the second hitch is made in the opposite direction from the first. A good fastening.

DIAMOND HITCH. This is a knot or series of knots used for fastening a load on a pack saddle. When made, the top part is in the form of a diamond. The cowboy speaks of "throwing a diamond." In fact, he "throws" all hitches, instead of "tying" them.

FIADOR KNOT. A very difficult knot, resembling the diamond knot in rope work, which is tied with four strands, two of which are closed.

HACKAMORE KNOT. This is the knot that attaches the fiador of the hackamore to the bosal. It is the common "bag knot," "bottle knot," or as it is sometimes called, the "beggarman's knot." The cowboy ties it doubled.

HALF HITCH. A loop which when placed over anything, such as a post, is "thrown" so that the part which is pulled is on top of the loop.

HITCHING KNOTS. These are important knots used in tying a lead rope or halter rope to a post. One type is a clove hitch, but it is finished off in such a fashion that the cowboy can jerk it loose quickly. Another type is a sailor's bowline knot, which also is made so it can be jerked loose quickly by the cowboy.

HONDA KNOT. This is in reality two knots, both overhand knots. First an overhand knot is made in the end of the rope, then another a short way back. The first knot is passed through the second and the second knot tightened, giving an eye or "honda" about two inches in diameter.

NECKERCHIEF KNOT. This is what the sailor calls a "square knot." It is tied in the ends of the neckerchief to hold it around the neck.

SQUAW HITCH. This is another type of hitch used on packsaddles. It is "thrown" like other hitches, instead of being tied. See CINCHA, FIADOR, HACKAMORE, HONDA, NECKERCHIEF, ROPE.

"Know Your Cans." A game played by cowboys in which they would recite from memory the exact words (with commas, periods, etc., in the right places) on the labels of canned milk or food stuff used at a ranch house. In the long winters, with nothing to do, and after thumbing through all the periodicals or books that might be around the ranch house, the cowboy would continue his reading by studying all written matter on can labels.

Lariat. A cowboy's rope. See ROPE.

Larrup. Molasses. Texans used it in place of sugar, even in coffee.

Larruping. A term meaning "great," "fine." Undoubtedly it came from larrup, the word for molasses.

Lasso. This term has come more and more to mean the cowboy's rope or lariat. However, in the old days the word "lasso" was used only as a verb, "to lasso." This followed the Mexican use of the Spanish word *lazar* (lath'ahr) which means much the same, "to lasso." Today usage has made lasso correct in meaning rope. See CATCH ROPE, ROPE.

Lass Rope. Another term for rope or lariat. See ROPE.

Latigo (lat'ee-go). A pliable leather strap used to fasten the cincha to the rigging ring on a saddle. A short latigo was used on the off, or right side, and a long one on the near, or left side. The latigo, with one end permanently fastened to the rigging ring, was passed twice through both

the cincha ring and the rigging ring and then tied at the rigging ring with a four-in-hand, or necktie knot—or what the sailor calls a "buntline hitch." The term "latigo" is also applied to soft, oiled leather. See CINCHA, KNOTS, LEATHER, RIGGING, SADDLE.

Layover. When a cowboy struck a town where he expected to stay a while, he called it a "layover." When he was forced to stop for a short time because of bad weather or some other delaying condition, he called it a "lay up."

Leader. A steer or cow that takes its place at the head of a herd of cattle. See CATTLE DRIVE.

Lead Poisoning. Cowboy lingo for the "sickness" a man got from a bullet.

Leather. The tanned or dressed skin or hide of an animal. There are two general ways of tanning leather, one by use of vegetable products such as the bark of certain trees, and the other by use of chemicals. The first is known as vegetable-tanned leather and is an "art leather," which can be decorated with carving, tooling, and stamping. The second is known as chemical- or chrome-tanned and is a general-utility leather. Some leather is alum tanned and heavily packed with oil and is very pliable and lasting.

Leather tanning was practiced before the recorded history of man. Pieces of leather articles, including caps and aprons, have been found in Egyptian tombs of 2,500 B.C. The process of tanning has changed little even today, although more tanning agents have been discovered. Oak bark still produces the best leather known, as it contains two kinds of tannin. However, because of the scarcity of this and other vegetable tanning agents, and particularly because of the length of time it takes to make leather with them, in this day of hustle and bustle the chrome or chemical process of tanning is encouraged. By use of such chemicals leather can be tanned in a much shorter period. Where, for instance, it would take six months by the older vegetable-tanning process, chrome leather can be made in six days.

Leathers are divided into hides, kips, and skins. "Hides" are pelts from the larger animals, like the cow, buffalo, horse, and elk. "Kips" come from undersized animals of the above class. "Skins" are obtained from such animals as calves, sheep, goats, deer, and reptiles, such as the snake. Thus it is incorrect to say "cow skin" or "goat hide." It is "cow hide" and "goat skin."

Cowboys' saddles usually are made from vegetable-tanned leather. This has been designated in the trade as "saddle leather" and generally is oak tanned. However, saddles not to be decorated by carving might be made from chemical-tanned leathers, and the more pliable leathers in latigos, reins, and headstalls frequently are chemical-tanned, oil-packed leather. See BELT, HEAD STALL, LATIGO, LEATHER BRAIDING, LEATHER CARVING, REINS, SADDLE.

Leather Braiding. The art of leather and rawhide braiding seems almost as old as the tamed horse. It has been associated with this noble animal since the days when the ancient Phoenicians invaded North Africa around 1600 B.C. The Phoenicians taught braiding to the Moors. The Moors carried it into Spain in the beginning of the eighth century. When Hernando Cortes brought the first horses to Mexico in 1520 he brought along, too, men skilled in leathercraft and braiding. Thus the western and southwestern cowboy learned braiding from Mexicans of early California and Texas.

In the old days the cowboy braided his quirts, bridles, reins, and other gear. Braiding went out of popularity for a time and horse gear was—and still is—decorated with silver ornaments. However, as this gear is heavy due to the weight of the increased ornamental metal, braided gear is again becoming popular.

The cowboy braids both with leather thongs and with rawhide strings or "whangs." The simpler forms of braids used are the "flat braid," "round braid," "slit braid," and "Turk's-head braid."

FLAT BRAID. In flat braiding the thongs are worked alternately from one side to the other. When the right-hand thong is brought toward the center over one thong,

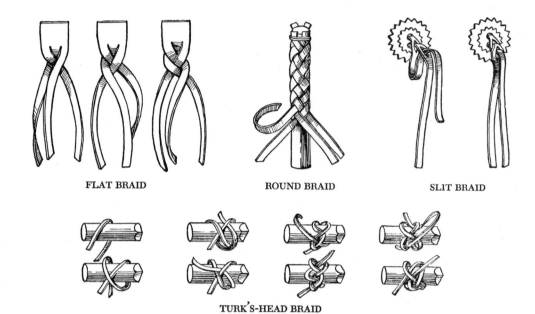

FLAT BRAID   ROUND BRAID   SLIT BRAID

TURK'S-HEAD BRAID

the left-hand thong is next brought toward the center over one thong. This is repeated, first one side and then the other, until the braid is complete. Flat braids are used in making belts.

ROUND BRAID. In the round braid the same method of working the thongs as used in the flat braid is employed, but in the round braid each thong is first passed around toward the rear and then brought forward. The round braid is used in making quirts, reins, and headstalls.

SLIT BRAID. The slit braid consists of pulling first one thong through a slit in another thong and then pulling the second thong back through a slit in the first one. This is used in attaching rosettes and conchas to saddles, as well as in making headstalls for hackamores.

TURK'S-HEAD BRAID. The Turk's-head braid is an endless wreath made of any of the flat braids. Only one thong is used. The Turk's-head braid is employed on the ends of quirt handles, to conceal the ends of thongs, for the start and finish of round braids, and for decoration of reins. See HEADSTALL, LEATHER, QUIRT, RAWHIDE, REINS, STRING, THONG.

Leather Carving. A method of decorating leather by outlining the design with a sharp knife and finishing it with saddle-stamping tools. Carved leather work is an old Moorish art which was introduced into Mexico by the Spanish soon after the invasion of Cortes. Originally it was applied principally to saddles, but it has become popular in decorating many serviceable types of articles, including belts, holsters, and handbags.

Only vegetable-tanned leathers which are unglazed are suitable for ornamental carving. The leather is first dampened and then saddle-soaped. It is allowed to dry to a point where no moisture is visible when the surface is pressed with the finger. A design drawn on paper is placed over the leather and the design traced through with a pencil or other sharp-pointed instrument. The impressions on the leather are then cut with a special knife, known as a "swivel cutter." The incision should be at right angles, straight down so there is no undercutting, and to a depth of about one-third the thickness of the leather. Next the background is stippled in with a stippling or background stamp, which is tapped with a long, heavy piece of wood, rather than with a hammer or mallet. The design is now planished or beveled by another tool, known as a "tap-beveler." Other tools are used for shading and veining. Sometimes the tools are heated to give more contrast to those parts which are depressed. However, if the leather is almost dry when worked, the depressed parts will be sufficiently dark to afford the proper contrast.

Most designs are composed of flowers, stems, and leaves which are intertwined. Some experts do not use paper designs but cut their own designs directly on the

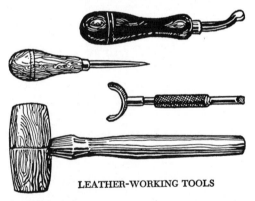

LEATHER-WORKING TOOLS

leather. Leather carving is not to be confused with leather tooling, where the design is not cut but pressed down with a modeling tool. See LEATHER, SADDLE STAMPING.

Leopard Horse. See APPALOOSA.

Levi's (lee'vyes). Blue denim overalls with pockets and seams put together with metal brads. In the old days these suggested

to the cowboy a laboring man or miner and he would not wear them. Today, however, they are dude ranch "musts." The story is that Levi Strauss, who manufactured the

originals, found that one of his agents on the Pacific Coast had used the metal brads at the suggestion of a miner. Miners carried heavy ore specimens in their pockets and the ordinary stitching would not hold. Strauss thought it a good idea and had all his pants made that way. Today the brads serve no purpose other than that of carrying on a tradition.

Line Camps. Outpost cabins or camps where cowboys live to watch over cattle and repair fences.

Line Rider. A cowboy who works out of a line camp. He has a regular territory to cover, watching over cattle and seeing to the repair of fences. He is different from the "outrider" who is something of a free-lance, or roamer. See BARBED WIRE, DUGOUT, OUTRIDER.

Loafer Wolf. Another name for the lobo or gray timber wolf. See WOLF.

Loco Weed. A poisonous weed, one variety of which is known as "marijuana," or the American hemp. When eaten by cattle and horses it will "loco" or "rattle" them. The effect of the weed is to cause the animals to die of starvation, first ruining their eyesight, and affecting their nervous systems as well as their brains. The animals at times become wild, or crazy. One species of the weed is known as the "purple loco" because of its purple flowers; and is sometimes called "woolly loco" from its hair leaves. Two other species have seed pods which rattle when dry. The term "loco" is from the Spanish word meaning "mad."

Lone Star. The five-pointed star of the flag of the Texas Republic. Texans made this star a part of the adornment of their equipment and demanded it on boot tops, saddles, bridles, and chaps. The manufacturers soon began putting it on all equipment and it became a standard part of ornamentation on cowboy dress.

There are several legends as to the origin of the Lone Star. One is that Henry Smith, elected governor of the provisional government of Texas when she declared her independence from Mexico in 1835, sealed his papers with the impression of a brass button on his coat, which had in relief a single star surrounded by an oak wreath. Another legend is that a Mrs. Venson presented a flag with the Lone Star on it to a Texas regiment, and the star was adopted for the first national standard of Texas. However, the first flag Texas had when she seceded

from Mexico was a naval flag with a single star and thirteen stripes, evidently borrowed from the United States. Later the stripes were discarded.

Long Hair. In the old West, a man who wore his hair long was called a "Long Hair." Cowboys did not wear their hair long from choice, and they were suspicious of those who did. Horse thieves, who had been fortunate enough to have only the top of an ear cut off instead of being hanged, sometimes wore long hair to conceal the "ear mark," and cowboys were thus suspicious of all long-haired men. Such Indian scouts as Buffalo Bill Cody wore their hair long through vanity, and Wild Bill Hickok, the famous marshal and gunfighter, had shoulder-length hair. But to call one of these men a "Long Hair," as the cowboy meant it, was to be answered, as likely as not, by the roar of a six-gun. See BAD MAN, CODY, HICKOK, HORSE STEALING.

Longhorn. The longhorn cow will always be the symbol of the cowboy and the old West. This rangy, fierce animal with a spread of horns which was sometimes six feet or more, was the wild type of the original Andalusian cattle brought to Mexico in the early 1500's. As wild cattle they crossed the Rio Grande and spread through the Southwest. They did not roam as far north as the horse, but only to the Red River, which now separates Texas and Oklahoma. By 1830 it was estimated that 100,000 cattle lived in Texas, four-fifths of them longhorns.

The first longhorns were driven to New Orleans in 1842, and eight years later others were driven to California. In 1859 they were driven across the Indian Territory to Colorado. In 1867 a drove of 600 longhorns went up the trail from Lockhart, Texas, to Abilene, Kansas, and this was the beginning of the great cattle drives which in the next seventeen years were to bring 5,000,000 longhorns up the trail for eastern markets and to stock northern ranches.

In later years ranchers began to breed out the longhorn by bringing in the Shorthorn, Hereford, Polled Angus, and other types of cattle from the East. The longhorn began to disappear. The government has, however, preserved the breed in the Wichita Mountains Wildlife Refuge.

The old-time cowboy liked the longhorn as he liked anything which would give him a good fight. Without the longhorn there would never have been the cowboy as we know him today. See CATTLE, CATTLE DRIVE, CHAPPARAL, COWBOY, MOSSY HORN.

Long Rider. An outlaw or bad man. The old Long Rider ballad went:
> *"Long riding, she's an easy life!*
> *A life that's full of fun.*
> *The prairie is our lodging house,*
> *The moon, it is our sun."* [1]

See BAD MAN.

Lope. A slow gallop. See GAIT.

Love Dance of the Catamounts. One of the wildest and noisest dances put on by celebrating cowboys.

[1] From *Triggernometry*, by Eugene Cunningham. Published by The Caxton Printers, Ltd., 1941.

Lynching. Hanging without waiting for the law to decide the fate of the victim. The word came from Charles Lynch of Virginia, who is said to have popularized this idea. Lynching was the fate of the horse rustlers and others who broke the unwritten laws of the Plains.

The lynching or "necktie party" rode the victim—his hands tied behind him—beneath the branch of the tree, and after tying the rope ran his horse out from beneath him, leaving him dangling. Or he might be stood up in a wagon and the wagon driven out from under him. Certain courtesies were given white men. They were hanged with "thirteen turns and a loop" in the hangman's knot. Others rated less turns. The victim was allowed to say a few last words. He often did—at length. One man is said to have complained because they made him "sit on this sorry old hoss, instead of that fine critter I stole." In departing, the members of the "necktie party" usually unloaded

their guns in the direction of the hanged man. But one man escaped death in this way, as a shot cut through the rope and he fell to the ground after the party left. See HORSE STEALING, VIGILANTE.

Maguey (mah'gway). See ROPE, ROPING.

"Makings." Tobacco and rice paper for making a cigarette. "Rolling cigarettes and smoking through his nose," is the way one writer described the cowboy. The cowboy usually rolls his cigarette with one hand. He holds the open rice paper in the "rolling" hand between the first and second fingers, with the thumb also pressing along the edge from beneath. Into the curled paper he pours his tobacco; then the forefinger distributes it evenly and is withdrawn, and the cigarette is rolled with the balls of the other fingers and the thumb. It is slid along the tongue, placed in the mouth, and lighted. Mexicans can roll a cigarette without wetting it, by folding over the end.

Some cowboys, to show their indifference, roll a cigarette while astride a bucking bronco. They lay the paper on the thigh, above the knee, dash in the tobacco, and roll it into shape with a quick sweep of the ball of the thumb. Then, with the finished cigarette between the fourth and fifth fingers of the "rolling" hand, the thumb and forefinger of that hand pinch one loop of the tobacco-sack's draw string, the cowboy seizes the other loop in his teeth, and whirls the sack closed. He then touches his tongue along the cigarette, pulls out a match, sweeps it over his tightened trouser leg, and the cigarette is going. Matches formerly used were sometimes the smelly Chinese punk matches, which came in little blocks of wood, each match split part way down so it could be broken off easily. "Makings" are carried in a pocket of the vest or shirt. See VEST.

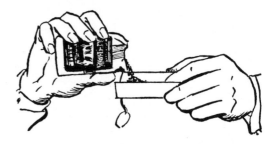

Man-Eater. Another term for a vicious horse, or "killer." He resorts to many tricks to unseat his rider, including the "throwback." See THROW-BACK.

Manila. Fiber for making rope. See ROPE.

Mare. A female horse that is used for

breeding purposes, commonly called "brood mare" on the range. While both male and female horses are called "cow horses" when used for range riding, the old-time cowboy seldom would ride a mare. Mares were for those who wanted extremely gentle horses—women and children. They caused too much diversion among the male horses in a remuda.

Martingale. A breast collar used with a saddle. One end of it passes between a

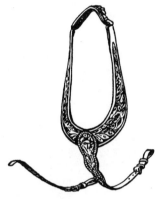

horse's legs and is attached to the cincha, the other to the bridle or noseband. It prevents a horse from throwing his head up.

Mast (or Mass) Crop. The crop from the acorns of the oak tree, used for fattening hogs and longhorn cattle. In California the old-time buckaroo ate bread made from acorn meal. See RAZORBACKS.

Maverick (mav′rick). A term for an unbranded calf wandering at large. The word was derived from the name of one Samuel Maverick, a Texas cattleman who refused to brand his cattle. Soon these "mavericks" were being branded by others, both the rustlers and rival cattle owners.

Mavericks were often "manufactured" by rustlers. They would kill the mother of a calf so they could claim that calf as a

maverick and place their own brand on it. The mother would, of course, carry a brand, and it was the common law of the range that calves should be branded with the same brand the mother bore. This type of rustler was said to be operating a "maverick factory."

While "maverick" usually applied only to cattle, in some districts it was a name for unbranded colts, too. However, such colts commonly were termed "slicks" or "slick ears." See RUSTLER.

Mecate (may-kah′tay). The twisted horsehair rope used on the hackamore for reins and lead rope. Cowboys call it "Mc-Carty." It is twenty-two feet in length and varies from three-eighths to five-eighths of an inch in diameter. It is secured on the bosal, just forward of the hackamore knot. See BOSAL, HACKAMORE, HORSEHAIR ROPE.

Medicine. The medicine of the old-time cowboy was simple. There were no doctors on the range, and few in the sparsely settled towns. Among the items in the medicine cabinet on a ranch might be found such things as Jamaica ginger, cathartic pills, and various patent medicines, as well as horse liniment. This liniment was diluted when used by humans. If a cowboy felt out of sorts, he might crawl into a "wickey-up" for a steam bath. When a cowboy was so sick he had to have medical care, he might be taken to a town in an Indian travois.

In the early days, if an arm or leg had to be amputated, it might be sawed off with a hand saw, the arteries tied up with horsetail hair, and the wound cauterized with a red-hot branding iron. In case there was no hot iron, some powder from a cartridge would be poured on the wound and ignited.

In the Southwest the Mexican *curanderas* (herb women) taught the cowboy the values of *remedios,* or herbs. These might be weed, bush, or root. For the bite of the rattlesnake the Mexicans used *poligala,* a type of milkweed, or the *cebadilla* (sneezewort); for a blood purifier they mashed and squeezed out the juices of wild watercress, lettuce, and endive; the common plantain weed gave a wash for sore eyes; and mullein was made into a poultice to cure sores, especially on horses. There was hardly a bush or tree or grass root the *curanderas* did not use in making their tonics, salves, and poultices. Even the violet and the rose, the wild radish, fennel, and catnip had their uses. See RATTLESNAKE, TRAVOIS, WICKEY-UP.

Menatha (men-ah'tha). The cowboy's way of saying the Spanish word *manada* (mah-nah'dah), or a band of horses ruled over by one stallion. The stallion's band of mares was sometimes called a "harem."

Mesquite (mes-keet'). A small, thorny tree of the bean family common to the Southwest. Horses and cows eat the beans and leaves of the mesquite.

Mex. A cowboy term meaning "false" or "no good." This term evidently grew out of the low value of Mexican currency.

Missouri Gate. The typical gate on a fenced-in ranch. It is a section of wire fence which can be opened by swinging out

one end of the section, to which is attached a free post. This post, when the gate is closed, is held in place by a loop of wire over a fixed post.

Morgan Horse. A breed of American horse which started in Vermont around 1800. Justin Morgan, a sturdy little horse, was named for Justin Morgan, a schoolteacher, who took him in payment of a debt. The product of Thoroughbred and Arabian breeding, he was a dark bay with black legs, mane, and tail. He stood fourteen hands high and weighed 950 pounds.

Justin Morgan was ridden and driven by men, women, and children, and he could out-walk, out-trot, and out-run all horses matched against him. The sire of a family of horses which have been recognized as a distinct breed, Justin Morgan was foaled in 1793 and died in 1821. His descendants for years held most of the records in harness racing.

The Morgan horse also is considered a utility horse for farm and ranch, and for driving and riding. As a saddle horse, ranchmen value him for his gentleness and intelligence and "cow sense." See ARABIAN, HORSE, THOROUGHBRED.

Morral (mor-r'rahl). Mexican term for nose bag. See Nose Bag.

Mossy Horns. A term for the wild long-horn cattle that lived in the chaparral or timber. They hid there during the day and grazed on the edge of the prairie during the night, always working back toward their hiding place, so that by daylight they would be close to the timber again. In this timber, especially in the South, the long Spanish moss which hung from the trees became entangled on their horns, and looked as if it actually were growing there.

Even when caught these animals would try to make for the timber again. To prevent this, cowboys used to sew up their eyes, and by the time the threads rotted and the eyelids could open, the "mossy horns" were far from their timber. Another method used to keep them from running toward timber was to tie them up by their own tails. The hairs of the tail were divided and knotted into a loop, then the tail was wrapped around the hind leg and the loop fastened in the split hoof. "Mossy horn" was also a term for a veteran cowman. See Cow Hunt, Longhorn.

Mule. An offspring of a jackass and a mare. Old-time cowboys rarely had anything to do with mules, although they were sometimes used around ranches and as pack animals. But still a cowboy might be forced to ride a mule when he did not have a horse. The man who drove mules was called a "skinner" or "mule skinner."

Mules sometimes become stubborn and refuse to move. They will never lead if looked directly in the eye, and to get them to go the man has to turn his back and walk away. When they balk, a small fire may then be built under them. They will usually move just far enough so the fire will be under the wagon or whatever they are

hitched to. A mule will "swell up" when saddled, and when the rider mounts he will pull in his belly so that the saddle will loosen and the rider finds himself "ridin' underneath." See Burro, Pack Horse.

Mule Skinner. The driver of mules. The old-time mule skinner usually was a tough character who had "private cuss words" of his own which he used in driving his charges. See Mule.

Muley Cow. A cow with very short horns. Sometimes called "mooley cow."

Muley Hat. A hat with a narrow brim.

Mustang. A term applied either to a wild horse or cow. Usually, however, it means a wild horse. The word is from the Mexican *mesteño* (mes-ten'yo), meaning an animal born in the mountains, which, while keeping its native characteristics, is wild and distrustful. The old-time mustang has become extinct. The wild horses that roam the unsettled regions of the West today are those that have become wild a second time, one might say. Mustangs are

95

also called "broomtails" and "fuzztails."

It was from the original bands of mustangs that Indians and early cowboys obtained their mounts. The mustangs of those days were fine horses, as the stallions heading each "menatha," or band of mares, fought off all inferior horses and kept the breeding standard high. Cowboys were always seeking the "Great White Mustang," the beautiful, proud horse with long flowing mane and tail who had the speed of the wind. This horse became a myth throughout the West and many reported having seen him and chased him, but none could capture him. He never died, and although he might disappear for years he would always come back to his home range. There are many stories of how fine mustangs had been captured, only to refuse food and die of broken hearts.

Custom, and later the law, said that all mustangs—horses or cattle—belonged to the ranch on which they grazed. A band of mustang horses needed about fifty square miles for grazing purposes. This was their home range, and a mustang born there would always return. Mustang colts were sometimes captured by the cowboys and raised on milch cows.

Some men made a business of capturing these wild horses. They were called "mustangers." They tried to drive the mustangs into blind corrals, they would walk them down, and as a last resort would "crease" them with rifle bullets.

In later years, the mustang became a nuisance, as these wild horses would lure other horses, especially mares, into their bands. As the grazing areas became more crowded, the mustangs were killed to conserve the grass. In later days mustangs have been rounded up by airplanes, and the bands driven over cliffs and killed. Many have been slaughtered for cat and dog food. See BLIND TRAP, CREASE, HORSE, WALK DOWN.

Near Side. The left side of a horse, on which the cowboy mounts.

Neckerchief. A handkerchief which a cowboy wears around his neck. It is also called "kerchief" or "bandanna." The neckerchief as worn by the working cowboy is folded diagonally to bring the two widely separated corners together and tied in a square knot around the cowboy's neck. The knot is in the back and the neckerchief hangs loosely. The triangular part in front can be pulled up over the nose and mouth like a mask when the cowboy is riding in the dust behind a herd of cattle, and it protects his face from sleet and bitter wind in the winter. Stagecoach robbers used neckerchiefs as masks, to conceal their faces.

The neckerchief is sometimes of silk, but the standard one is red bandanna cotton. The old-time cowboy never wore a white neckerchief as it reflected light and could be seen for great distances. White also showed dirt. The red bandanna, manufactured for Negro women in the South, was always to be had, and the cowboy soon began to prefer it to any other color.

The big flowing neckerchief held by a slide came in with the movie cowboy and the dude ranch. The slide is a ring or fastening used to hold the ends of the neckerchief together. Slides used on the big flowing neckerchiefs of the comic character cowboy, the movie cowboy, and the dude are made from braided leather knots, skulls of small birds, metal rings, etc. See KNOTS.

Necking Up. Cowboy term for an operation in which four or five wild horses are tied abreast so they can be driven more easily.

Neck Rope. A rope which passes around the horse's neck and keeps him head-on to the calf or steer after it has been caught with the lariat. The lariat passes from the saddle horn through the neck

rope. Sometimes after a rider has dismounted to tie up the roped steer, the horse will "spook" or stampede and drag the steer behind him. The neck rope prevents him from turning. It is commonly used in rodeo roping. See RODEO, ROPING.

Necktie Party. See LYNCHING.

Needle Gun. An old-fashioned rifle or carbine in which the powder charge was fired by a long pin or needle. Instead of this firing pin striking the cap at the base of the cartridge, it penetrated the cartridge just in the rear of the bullet and ignited the powder there. This was the type of carbine with which William F. Cody won his name "Buffalo Bill." It was a .53 caliber United States Army Schroeder carbine, which made an ideal buffalo gun. Buffalo Bill called his carbine "Lucretia Borgia," because of its murderous qualities. See BUFFALO GUN, CODY.

Nester. A homesteader. "Nesters" were usually farmers. They received government grants of land and commonly settled near water. They would fence off watering places, which legally was their right, but this kept the range cattle out. In the beginning there were many bitter wars between cowboys and nesters. The coming of the nester was the beginning of the end of the old-time cowboy. But many a cowboy befriended nesters and their families who had come West with high hopes, and found themselves set down in the middle of the dry plains by "freighters," where they had no fuel or food. See FREIGHTERS, GRANGER.

Nicknames. Nicknames or "handles" were popular in the West. It was considered impolite to ask a stranger's full name or to look too closely at the brand on an animal. How did a man get his nickname? Usually because of something he had done, or from the place where he made a reputation, or because of something about his looks or actions. For instance, "Bill" was used in many combinations as a nickname. There was Pecos Bill, Billy the Kid, Wild Bill, Buffalo Bill, Bill of the Lazy A Outfit, Flat-Nosed Bill, Long Bill, Big-Foot Bill, Texas Bill, and so on. A man might be called Alkali Ike because he was hard like alkali water, or he might be the Sundance Kid because he came from Sundance. As a Westerner explained to a tenderfoot in warning him not to try to find out a cowboy's full name, "He most likely has given a first-class funeral to the rest of his name, and I wouldn't ask him for no resurrections." See HANDLE.

Nighthawk. The night herder of the saddle horses. The nighthawk drives the wood wagon in the daytime. See ROUNDUP.

Night Herding. Guarding cattle on the trail at night. For the ordinary herd there were usually two night herders. They would ride around the sleeping or resting herd in opposite directions. If one went clockwise, the other went counter-clockwise. Night herders usually sang while they rode, as this was supposed to give the cattle confidence.

These men were great students of the stars. As usually they were without timepieces, they would "tell time" by the Great Dipper, which was called by the Mexicans "the Clock of the Yaquis." The Great Dipper swings around the North Star every twenty-four hours. Night herders going on duty would note carefully the position of the "clock's hands," the Alpha and Beta of the Great Dipper, in its relation to the North Star. When it had marked off a third of the night, the night herders figured their watch was up. See CATTLE DRIVE, COWBOY SONGS, STAMPEDE.

Night Horses. Saddle horses kept near a ranch house at night in case one is wanted in a hurry.

No Man's Land. A desolate section of land once in the Indian Territory and now a part of Oklahoma. It was bordered by the Cimarron River and was a refuge for cattle rustlers, horse thieves, and outlaws.

Nooning. The stopover at noontime for rest and food. The old-time cowboy would say, "We made our nooning on the banks of the Brazos."

Norther. The Texas term for blizzard. See BLIZZARD.

Nose Bag. This is a round, bucketlike feed bag placed over a horse's nose and held on the animal's head with a strap. It is dangerous around water, for if a horse tries to drink while wearing a nosebag he may

fill the bag with water and drown himself. The Mexican word for nosebag, *morral*, also was sometimes used by some of the southwestern cowboys.

Off Side. The right side of a horse. The left side is called the "near side." Indians mount a horse on the off side, while cowboys get aboard on the left side, or the near side. See NEAR SIDE.

On the Prod. Fighting mad. May be said of a man or an animal.

Open Range. The vacant or unfenced land of the plains and prairies of the West and Southwest which was open to everyone, and where grass and water were free. In the days of the open range the cattlemen cared little about ownership of land, unless it was the site of their ranch buildings. Their great herds of cattle had unlimited grazing areas; they intermingled and sometimes drifted hundreds of miles before severe storms. But there was a general roundup once a year, usually in early spring at a time set by agreement of cattlemen in certain sections. Often there was also a second roundup in the fall. Cattle were sorted out, and calves branded with the brand carried by their mothers.

While most ranchers would have representatives to claim their cattle at a roundup, the unwritten "code of the range" was that a cattleman brand not only his own calves but place the proper brand on those of all other ranchers. If a calf was over a year old and not following a branded cow, it was considered a "maverick," and the cattleman could place his own brand on it. Some cattlemen sought to evade the code of the range by rounding up cattle earlier than the time set, and thus brand mavericks before their neighbors had the opportunity. But later cattlemen's associations were formed to stop this practice, as well as rustling and all types of illegal branding. Brands had to be registered at the county seats, and cattle owners carried hundreds of brands in their heads. Usually they could tell the ownership of a branded cow on sight.

While the open range often was spoken of as the "cow country," many ranchers raised only horses. But they would speak of having "a horse ranch in the cow country."

With the coming of homesteaders to the West following the War between the States, many cattlemen found their water supplies cut off, as these "nesters" would usually locate their farms near streams or springs and then fence them in. In some instances they would divert water sources by irrigation ditches. At first cattlemen cut the fences and tried by threats to frighten the farmers away. But as the numbers of farmers increased and more and more water supplies were fenced in, many bloody "wars" resulted between ranchers and farmers. The farmers were within their rights, however, and soon cattlemen began to take up ownership of land and fence it in, too.

The cattlemen also considered the coming of sheep to the open range as a scourge. They claimed that sheep polluted the watering places and that no cow or horse would drink there after them, and that they also killed off the grass by nibbling it to the roots. By 1887 all ranchers had begun to feel the pinch of wire fences and the open range began to disappear. See Barbed Wire, Cattle King, Nester, Rep, Roundup, Rustler War, Sheep.

Orejana (or-ay-hah'nah). The California buckaroo's term for unbranded colt or "slick." See Slick.

Ornery. Low, mean, vile. The cowboy's favorite word for something he does not like. A coyote is an "ornery critter."

Outfit. A term meaning people living together and working at the same thing. A ranch and the cowboys working on it is called an "outfit." A group of people traveling together is an "outfit." The word is used also to refer to the things a cowboy owns. See Ranch.

Outlaw. A spoiled horse. Such horses are tricky, and the cowboy never knows what they are going to do. They also have remarkable bucking ability when they settle down to it. "Outlaw" also means bad man, or desperado. See Bad Man, Killer, Throw-back.

Outrider. A cowboy of the old days who made a general tour of inspection on the range or ranch to look over stock, see that they were on good grazing ground, and in good health. See Line Rider.

Overland Stage. A passenger, mail, and express company which ran stagecoaches from Atchison, Kansas, to Placerville, California, a distance of 1,913 miles. The Overland Stage Company was formed in 1862 by Ben Holladay, who operated local stage lines in the Colorado region, after he had purchased the Central Overland California & Pike's Peak Express Company. This company had run a stage line from Independence, Kansas, to Placerville, California, along the route of the Oregon Trail. The Holladay Company, however, only followed the Oregon Trail to Julesburg, Colorado, and then passed through Denver and thence to Salt Lake City and Placerville.

The route was divided into three great divisions, each of which was divided into three minor divisions. There were 153 stations, twelve to fifteen miles apart, known as "swing stations," and each fifty miles there was a "home station." At these latter stations passengers could obtain meals and lodging if desired. Horses were changed every twenty-five to thirty-five miles at the "swing stations," or sooner if necessary. Drivers were changed at the same time as the horses, but messengers, or the men who "rode shotgun" on the stagecoaches, were changed only about once every 200 miles. When trouble with Indians or road agents was expected, more than one messenger might ride with the stage.

The stage line ran passenger service six days a week. On Mondays, only a "messenger coach" carrying express left the east and west terminals. Fares from Atchison to Denver were $75; to Salt Lake City, $150; and to Placerville, $225. Each passenger was allowed twenty-five pounds of baggage and was charged $1.00 a pound for excess baggage. During the War between the States the fares more than doubled, so that at one time it cost $525 to ride from Atchison to Placerville.

The record stage run was fourteen miles in fifty-two minutes. One of the Denver runs, of 635 miles, was made in four and one-half days. Ben Holladay, to keep an important engagement in the East, broke all records in 1864 when he made the run from Placerville to Atchison in twelve days and two hours, averaging six and two-thirds miles an hour with all stops included. The trip cost him $20,000, but he "considered the money well spent." Wells Fargo & Company bought the lines in 1866, but kept shortening the distance of the run as the Kansas Pacific Railroad pushed west.

Another stage line, known as the Butterfield Overland Mail, ran from St. Louis, Missouri, to El Paso, Texas, and through Arizona to Los Angeles and on to San Francisco, a distance of 2,795 miles. See STAGECOACH.

Over the Jump. A cowboy term used to mean "killed."

Pack Horse. A horse equipped with a packsaddle. It is usually the "plug" of the outfit. The old-time cowboy in moving his belongings from one place to another commonly used a pack horse. Burros and mules are good pack animals for rough country. See BURRO, MULE, PACKSADDLE.

Packing In. Journeying into a section with pack animals.

Packsaddle. A simple form of saddle used on a pack horse. It consists of two sides, lined with sheep wool, which fit over

the horse's back. At the top are two cross-trees to which the load is lashed. Sometimes containers known as "kyacks" are lashed on each side. The packsaddle is usually double-rigged, with two cinchas or bellybands, as well as a breast collar and a breech or hip strap. A thick pad is used beneath the saddle, which carries about seventy-five to ninety pounds on each side.

Another form of packsaddle is the *aparejo* (ah-par-ay'ho), a stuffed leather pad with a broad cincha. Kyacks cannot be carried on this type of packsaddle. The diamond hitch, double and single, and the squaw hitch are used in securing the load. See PANNIER.

Pads. Felt or woolen blankets used beneath saddles and packsaddles. Fancy pads are known as "coronas." See CORONA, SADDLE BLANKET.

Pad Saddle. A type of saddle used in the old days by Plains Indians. It was made from two pieces of soft, dressed buffalo, deer, elk, or antelope hide, stuffed with hair and sewed together in a sort of hourglass shape. These saddles weighed about three pounds and were held on by a cincha or bellyband of rawhide from two to four inches wide.

Paint Pony. See CALICO HORSE, PINTO.

Palomino (pal-oh-mee′noh). This beautiful horse is sometimes called "the golden one." The old name was "California sorrel." The horse is golden-colored with a white mane and tail. The true Palomino is defined by the Palomino Horse Association as "a horse carrying the color of a newly minted U.S. gold coin, with mane and tail a natural white. He shall have a good head, stand alert on well-set legs with good withers and a short-straight back, and have a good natural tail carriage. He shall stand approximately 15.2 hands high and have an approximate weight of 1,100 pounds at maturity."[1] White-booted feet are permissible.

The Palomino is not accepted as a recognized breed of horse, but is a color within various breeds already recognized. The Palomino was bred in California before 1848. It is the favorite mount of movie actors and a spectacular horse in a parade.

There are many stories about the origin of this horse. One is that a foreman at a California mission around 1800 offered a prize for the best horse in the country, and a cinnamon-colored yearling with a white mane and tail was selected. This one be-

[1] From a statement of the Palomino Horse Association.

came the father of all Palominos. Others believe the Palomino came from the Spanish horses which were descendants of the Barb and Arabian horses. The early Palominos were highly prized, and a Spanish don would present one as a gift when his daughter was married. Today Arabian Thoroughbreds are used in carrying on the type. See ARABIAN, HORSE.

Pannier (pan′yer). A container (either a bag or a box) adapted to be slung on a

packsaddle, for carrying supplies and clothing. The bag or sack pannier is a flat, oblong leather or canvas bag which is used for transporting nonbreakable articles. The box pannier is a flat, narrow box covered with rawhide with the hair usually left on. Some box panniers are covered with canvas and are used for carrying breakable articles and kitchen gear. See PACKSADDLE.

Panola (pah-noh′lah). The cowboy's way of saying *pinole* (pee-noh′lay), the Mexican term for ground, parched, spiced and sweetened maize or Indian corn. It was carried by the old-time cowboy to eat as a thirst-quencher.

Parada (par-ah′dah). A term used by the buckaroos of California for a main herd of cattle. Sometimes pronounced "peratha" by the cowboy.

Parfleche (pahr′flesh). A folded rawhide container; also, the rawhide from which the container was made. Parfleches were the suitcases and the trunks of the plains. See PANNIER, RAWHIDE.

Peace-Maker. See COLT.

Peccary (peck'a-ree). The American wild pig found in Texas. The peccary, which stands about three feet high and has a white band around its neck, can be tamed. Unlike the domestic pig, the peccary gives birth to only two offspring. The peccary is an enemy of the rattlesnake and will kill and eat the reptile. Sometimes it is called "javelina." It is not to be confused with the razorback hog. See RATTLESNAKE, RAZORBACKS.

Pecos Justice. A "hit-or-miss" type of western justice. The name came from the decisions given by "Judge" Roy Bean of Pecos County, Texas. The large painted sign on "Judge" Bean's saloon read, "Law West of the Pecos." It was said of him that he was a "teacher and barber and mayor; he was cook and old-shoe mender, sometimes preacher and bartender, and it cost two-bits to have him cut your hair." When an Austin City dude came to his place and complained about being charged nine dollars for a drink, the "justice of the peace"

fined him one dollar for contempt of court, which meant he got no change from his ten-dollar bill. Once, when a dead Chinese

was found with $150 and a .45 caliber Colt on his corpse, the "Jedge" fined him the $150 "for carrying concealed weepons."

Peg Pony. See CUTTING HORSE.

Pelado (pay-lah'do). An insulting term for a lazy or worthless Mexican. The word is Mexican, meaning a person who is uncultured and uncouth. As used by the southwestern cowboy, it meant about the same as the term "poor white trash" means in the South.

Pelon (pee-lon'). A gift made by a storekeeper after a big purchase. It was usually a piece of candy, a cigar, or some small item. An old-time cowboy in purchasing supplies from a store was always on the lookout for his "pelon." This is from the Mexican *pilon* (pee-lon'), a gratuity, or that given in addition to the buyer by the seller.

Pemmican (pem'i-kan). A term for dried meat, or jerked meat, which was pounded into a powder and then mixed with the melted fat and marrow. The cowboy learned the use of pemmican from the Indians, who made it from buffalo meat or deer meat. It was packed in bags of hide and stored for winter use.

In choice pemmican great care was used in the selection and drying of the meat, and a good deal of fat and marrow was used. The food, stored in bales, was highly prized and remained sweet and good as long as it was kept dry. The Red River half-breeds dealt in this meat extensively. Fried bacon, covered with its own fat, can be preserved in the same fashion. See CHUCK, JERKED MEAT.

Piebald. A horse that is covered with spots of black and white.

Piggin' Strings. Ropes used in tying an animal's legs after it has been roped and thrown. See Roping.

Pilgrim. A newcomer to the West. First applied to imported cattle and later to humans. See Tenderfoot.

Pinto (pin'to). The term for a horse which is colored yellow, black, and white. From the Mexican *pinto* (peen'to) mean-

ing a mixture of several colors. In Texas such horses are known as "paint ponies." Some pintos are found with crystal-like eyes called "glass eyes." This does not affect the sight of the horse and such a horse is often highly prized. See Calico Horse, Horse.

Pinwheeling. A kind of fancy gunplay. The six-gun is tossed into the air so that it turns end over end and drops into the hand in a position for action. See Pistol.

Pistol. The hand gun of the cowboy, commonly of .44 or .45 caliber. It might be the Colt "Peace-Maker," the Remington "Frontier," or the Smith & Wesson .44 caliber "American," but it was usually known by the name of "Colt." All pistols were called "Colts." The cowboy also gave such names to his pistol as "six-gun," "six-shooter,"

"shooting iron," "talking iron," "blue lightning," "flame thrower," "lead pusher," and "hog-leg." Despite the fact that it was a six-shooter, it was rarely loaded with more than five cartridges, the hammer of the gun resting over the empty chamber.

Though the Remington and the Smith & Wesson were fairly popular, the cowboy's gun was more often the Colt .44 or .45 caliber, which weighed two and one-quarter pounds, was a single-action, and had an eight-inch barrel. The cowboy preferred the single-action to the double-action as he liked simplicity, and he figured such a gun was less likely to get out of order. Also, while the double-action pistol might prove faster on the first shot, the cowboy could empty his gun faster with a single-action, especially when fanning. Still, fanning was possible with both the single-action and the double-action. The cowboy's gun had no shiny, nickle-plated parts, as he wanted nothing which would reflect the sun.

The six-gun served many purposes. The old-time cowboy could light a fire by taking some powder from a cartridge and shooting at it, just so the edge of the flame from the muzzle ignited the loose powder. He could open a can of tomatoes by shooting along the top.

The cowboy never "slapped leather," or let his hand come near his gun butt unless he intended drawing the gun and using it.

There was no such thing as "fingering his gun" while engaged in an argument. He removed the gun before sitting down to the dinner table, and when he went to a neighbor's ranch he took off his belt with holster and gun and hung it over the horn of his saddle before going inside the ranch house. But when calling on his girl, he did not remove the weapon, as he calculated such "artillery" impressed the fair sex.

After many shootings and killings in the wild cow towns of the West, the wearing of the six-gun became unpopular. Most town marshals made the cowboys check their guns at his office. As cowboys felt "plumb naked" without a gun, some would carry "hide-outs." Several of the cattlemen's associations ruled that cowboys even on the range should not wear guns unless in the vicinity of hostile Indians or cattle rustlers. See BORDER SHIFT, COLT, CROSS DRAW, DOUBLE-ACTION, FANNING, HIDE-OUT, HOLSTER, PINWHEELING, QUICK-DRAW, ROAD AGENT'S SPIN, ROLLING, SINGLE-ACTION.

Pitchin'. Bucking. A term used by Texans, who also called bucking "cayusin'." See BUCKING.

Plumb. One of the cowboy's favorite adjectives, meaning "fully," "completely."

Poker-Chip Draw. This was a practice draw, but unlike "dry shooting," the six-gun was actually fired. The gunfighter placed a poker chip or other small object on the back of his gun hand. He raised this hand shoulder high, turned it so the poker chip slid off, and then with the same hand withdrew his gun in time to shoot at the chip before it hit the ground. Harvey (Kid Curry) Logan, a notorious outlaw, could, it was said, fire three times before the chip landed. See DRY SHOOTING, QUICK-DRAW.

Polled. Hornless. Applied to such cattle as the polled Angus, which has no horns.

Pommel. The saddle horn. See HORN.

Poncho (pon'cho). A blanket or oiled cloth with a hole in the middle for the head. Mexicans used the woolen sarape with a

thirteen-inch hole in the center and called it *jorongo.* If of oiled cloth, it was termed *manga de hule.* See SARAPE.

Pony. The cowboy term for a saddle horse. It did not mean a small horse but was applied to all saddle horses. See HORSE.

Pony Express. A mail service established April 3, 1860, between St. Joseph, Missouri, and Sacramento, California, a distance of 1,966 miles, through rugged and hostile country. The Pony Express used the stagecoach stations already established along this route, which today is almost exactly followed by the lines of the Union Pacific Railroad. No more exciting event took place that year than the beginning of this fast mail service. Riders left Sacramento and St. Joseph on the same day and at the same hour. New York newspapers carried big stories. At stations along the way, people pulled hairs from the tails of the horses to keep as souvenirs.

Pony Express riders always traveled light. The letters, written on finest tissue paper, were wrapped in oiled silk, then placed in a leather pouch which was locked and sealed and strapped to the rider's side. No rider was allowed to carry more than twenty pounds of mail. Postage was $5.00 a half ounce. There were 80 riders, 400 horses, and 300 station-keepers and assistants at the 190 stations along the route. The riders, who were supposed to make 250 miles a day, averaging about ten miles an hour, changed horses every fifteen miles. They were relieved at intervals and rode day and night.

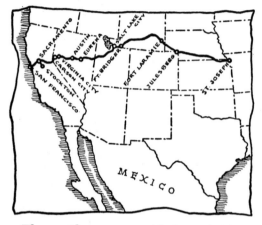

These riders were paid from $120 to $125 a month, good salaries for this period. The first trip was made in ten days. Sometimes trips were made in eight days, but the average was nine days. President Buchanan's last presidential message was carried in December, 1860, in a little over eight days. But the record time was made when President Lincoln's inaugural address was carried in March, 1861, in seven days and seventeen hours.

Mark Twain, in *Roughing It,* gives this picture of a Pony Express rider as seen from a stagecoach which the rider passes: "Presently the driver exclaims, 'Here he comes!' Every neck is stretched and every eye strained. Away across the endless prairie a black speck appears against the sky. In a second or two it becomes a horse and rider, rising and falling, rising and falling—sweep-

ing towards us nearer and nearer—growing more and more distinct, more and more sharply defined—nearer and still nearer, and still nearer, and the flutter of hoofs comes faintly to the ear—another instant a whoop and a hurrah from our upper deck, a wave of the rider's hand, but no reply, and man and horse burst past our excited faces, and go swinging away like a belated fragment of a storm."

On October 21, 1861, when the first telegraphic communication was made between the East and West, the Pony Express lost its usefulness and soon went out of business.

Many famous cowboys and plainsmen rode in this service, including Buffalo Bill Cody and Pony Bob Haslam. The service needed brave and hardy men, as they rode through dangerous territory. Sometimes they found their relief riders had been killed or wounded by Indians or outlaws, and then they would have to ride on to the next stage. This happened once to Pony Bob Haslam, who rode 380 miles and was in the saddle for thirty-six hours straight. At one time newspapers carried this advertisement:

WANTED. — YOUNG, SKINNY, WIRY FELLOWS NOT OVER 18. MUST BE EXPERT RIDERS, WILLING TO FACE DEATH DAILY. ORPHANS PREFERRED. WAGES $25 PER WEEK. APPLY, CENTRAL OVERLAND PONY EXPRESS.

The regular schedule of the Pony Express beat the Overland Stage by two days, and on its record-breaking run beat the stage by five days. See CODY, OVERLAND STAGE.

Pony-Express Mount. A flying or running mount in which the rider does not use the stirrup, but catches the horn and is jerked into the saddle as the horse starts. It was used by Pony Express riders.

Porcupine. A rodent with stiff, coarse hair and long, sharp spines, called quills, found in many parts of the West. The idea that a porcupine could "shoot his quills" was commonly believed by the cowboys. The animal was a nuisance as it was fond of oiled leather, especially the latigos of saddles, and would chew these whenever it got a chance. Cowboys often were called on to pick the sharp quills from horses' hocks, and dogs seemed to get plenty of them in their noses. Indians valued the porcupine quills. They colored and flattened them and used them for decoration

on warriors' moccasins, quivers, and vests. Squaws were clever in working them into elaborate and colorful patterns.

Post. This is what the cowboy terms "fancy riding" when a horse is trotting. It means to rise and fall in the saddle in motion with the horse. This shows "daylight" between saddle and rider, and to a cowboy this means bad riding. The cowboy's horse usually broke into a lope from a walk. If it trotted, which was rare, the cowboy "sat it out," but did not post. See GAIT.

Postage Stamp. A cowboy term for the small, light-weight English-type saddle. It is also called a "kidney pad."

Pot Shot. Hitting more than one person or animal with one shot. In the old West it meant a shot which would get the most game for the pot. An Indian, stalking deer, would come upon a group of them, and in maneuvering around so that he could kill more than one with a "pot shot," was apt to frighten them away. Later "to take a pot shot" at something meant to fire at random.

Prairie. A level or rolling plain without trees but with coarse grass and rich soil. In the United States the prairies extend from southern Michigan and western Ohio over Illinois, Indiana, Missouri, Wisconsin, and Minnesota, and west of the Missouri River to the foothills of the Rocky Mountains.

The terms "plains" and "prairie" were used one for the other in the old days, and authorities speak of "Plains Indians" and "Prairie Indians" when meaning the same Indians. However, the plains comprised the higher, drier areas westward to the Rockies. The plains were more level than the prairie and usually the ground was poorer.

Prairie Chicken. A game bird, with mottled plumage, smaller than the domestic chicken. It is a species of grouse, and good to eat. It is sometimes called "prairie hen" or "sage hen."

Prairie Dog. The little prairie dog is a familiar sight to the cowboy. These rodent-like creatures live in underground "towns," and how they always keep "fat and sassy" is something that has long puzzled the cowboy. They live mainly on the roots of grass. Horses shy around the prairie-dog towns because a leg can be broken by stepping into one of their holes.

In extreme cold weather the prairie dog community is a strange one, as usually the rattlesnake and the squinch owl then join the prairie dog family in their holes. But it is not a happy family. The rattlesnake, when the mother and father prairie dogs are absent, eats the young prairie dogs, but

the parents never seem to miss the young ones. However, the squinch owl likes to eat young rattlesnakes, and this evens things up somewhat. The little owl, called by the Indians "dancing owl," even attacks larger rattlesnakes, waiting for them to come out of the holes and then seizing them by the neck and choking them to death.

The prairie dog has a sharp little bark. Cowboys claim that if one is shot, in his last dying effort he will leap into his hole. See Rattlesnake, Squinch Owl.

Prairie Fire. This was a terror of the open range. All hands turned out to fight a prairie fire for if not stopped it would destroy everything in its path, and might sweep for miles across the plains. Cowboys riding along could sniff a prairie fire long before they could see the smoke. They would ride toward the fire through the hundreds of frightened animals who were fleeing before it—deer, antelope, wolves, rabbits, horses, cattle, and buffaloes. Where there was no water at hand—and this was nearly always the case—the cowboys would kill cattle, split them open, and drag the carcasses over the path of the fire. Two long

ropes were tied to a carcass, and one cowboy would ride on one side of the fire and another on the other side. Smaller fires were beaten out with fresh hides and blankets. In some cases a backfire would be started to burn a furrow before the oncoming fire. During a high wind it was almost impossible to stop a prairie fire.

As a safeguard against prairie fires ranchers would encircle their ranges with a wide belt of plowed-up earth.

Prairie Schooner. The name given the wagons of the western immigrants. However, the typical prairie schooner was said to have been built first by Gail Borden, an editor and the inventor of condensed milk, who went to Texas with Stephen B. Austin. Borden constructed the wagon so it would actually be a boat on wheels and could be floated across streams.

Prickly Pear. See Cactus.

Pulling Down. Getting the drop on another armed man. See Getting the Drop.

Pulling Leather. To touch or hang onto the saddle while riding a bucking bronc. "Pulling leather" will disqualify a rider in a rodeo contest. See Rodeo.

Puncher. A shortened form of cowpuncher, meaning a cowboy. See Cowpuncher.

Quarter Horse. This horse is sometimes called "the poor man's race horse." One old-timer in describing the Quarter Horse said, "Ma'am, a Quarter Hoss is a short-winded, low-geared race hoss."

The Texans take credit for having developed the Quarter Horse. One account is that it originated in that state through the crossing of a Thoroughbred stallion and a black pony mare. But apparently this type of horse originated in Virginia and the Carolinas before the Revolution, and was used as a race horse for the quarter mile, hence its name, Quarter Horse. The Quarter Horse, while not a breed, is divided into three types: the racing type, with many registered as Thoroughbreds; the bulldog type, something like the ordinary draft horse, and the practicing ranch type. While a sprinter, the Quarter Horse is an excellent polo pony and a top ranch horse. He is valued as a cutting horse and one with "cow sense." See CUTTING HORSE, HORSE.

Quick-Draw. A term for the lightning-like withdrawal of the six-gun from the holster and getting it into action. Everything about the holster, method of wearing the gun belt, and the position of the gun

butt was planned to make the quick-draw possible. The belt hung loose so that in reaching down for the gun butt the cowboy's arm was slightly curved. He found this correct position himself by practice. There was no flap on the holster, nothing which would be in the way of the gun.

The quick-draw was all-important in gunfighting, where a split second meant life or death. While riding, the gun was commonly hung from the left side, butt forward, for the cross draw. If two guns were worn, one on each side, the gunfighter crossed his arms in the cross-arm draw.

Gunfighters invented many ways to get their guns out more quickly. There was a special vest, with pockets as holsters; unholstered guns were hung from swivels on the belt, and others in open-toed swivel holsters. "Hide-outs" were common. A gunfighter might wear one gun in plain view but when he went into action it was the hide-out which flashed from beneath his vest or from the end of his sleeve. Cowboys practiced the quick-draw and aiming in their spare moments. This was called "dry shooting." See BAD MAN, CROSS DRAW, DRY SHOOTING, GETTING THE DROP, HIDE-OUT, HOLSTER, PISTOL, POKER-CHIP DRAW.

Quick Stop. Cowboys speak of the quick stop made by a saddle horse as "slammin' on the brakes." The horse comes

to a stop from any speed. He gathers his hind legs beneath him, with head down, and slides on his hind feet to a stop. This is important in the cutting horse and rope horse, as they must stop quickly. The latter prepares for the quick stop the minute he sees the cowboy's right (or lariat) hand go up. See Cutting Horse, Roping.

Quile. (kwyle). To curl up as in sleep.

Quirt. A short, loaded whip. The whip, as well as the word itself, is of Mexican origin. In Mexico they call it *cuarta* (kwar'-tah). Old-time cowboys sometimes referred to the quirt as "quisto." The quirt commonly has a braided rawhide stock, from twelve to fifteen inches long; a leather loop or wristband about six inches long, and two thongs, known as the lash, on the other end. The lash is the same length as the handle or stock. The rawhide is sometimes braided over a core made from a tapered shot-filled leather bag.

The weighted quirt is a deadly weapon, and the cowboy sometimes uses the heavy end on a horse that rears in the throw-back. He strikes the horse between the ears and the blow may kill him. In breaking a horse the quirt is freely used. Some quirts are highly decorated with Spanish woven knots, called "buttons," and split leather tasseling, known as "frills." When

not in the cowboy's hand the quirt is hung from the saddle horn. See Bust, Button, Frill, Leather Braiding, Throw-back.

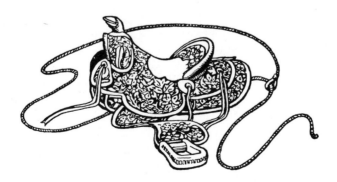

Railbird. A cowboy who sits on the top of a rail of a corral fence as an onlooker. See CHUTE ROOSTERS.

Rake. To spur. In rodeo riding contests the cowboy rakes his mount from the shoulders to the cincha on the first five bucks, and then from the cincha to the rump in the last five bucks. The purpose of this is so the cowboy cannot hang onto the cincha with his spur buckhooks. Judges watch carefully to see that contestants rake. Raking the horse with the spurs in this way is also called "cowboying"—something the working cowboy never does. See BUCK-HOOK, RODEO.

Ranch. An establishment in the cattle country consisting of buildings, land, livestock, and the owner and his employes. The term is derived from the Mexican *rancho,* and in the early days the southwestern ranch was a "ranche." The word ranch sometimes is used just to mean the ranch house, or the "shack," or main building. A ranch might be called an "outfit," or a "spread," and along the Pacific Coast in the old days the ranch might have been a mission carrying on ranching activities.

Early ranch houses in the North usually were constructed of hewn and squared logs, chinked with clay, and the doors and windows tightly fitted because of the cold winters. In the South they were of unpainted boards, and along the Border might have been adobe structures. In some places ranch houses were no more than dugouts, frequently built into a hill. The main building of the ranch house sometimes consisted of one large room with cowboys' bunks lined around the walls and with rows of pegs for saddles, bridles, lariats, and other gear. There was a fireplace as well as a cookstove in houses in the colder sections. In the center of the room was a long table with crude chairs. In some cases the cook's shack was an adjoining building and the cowboys occupied a separate building known as a "bunk house." There were no fences. Usually there was a barn with an open shed, a hitching bar, and several corrals or "round pens."

Ranch houses generally were built near springs or streams of water. If not, there would be a well and possibly a large "tank" dug into the ground and lined with clay to hold rainwater. No ranch in the days of the open range had gardens or grain fields.

During the reign of the cattle kings and when eastern and foreign capital flowed into the cattle country, the ranches became more up-to-date and some were even luxurious. The wealthy cattle kings spared no expense and imported furnishings and ranch equipment. Today some ranches offer facilities equal to fine hotels.

Before the days of barbed wire the boundaries of the grazing lands of a ranch would be dotted with "line camps," called "sign camps" in Utah and regions west. Line riders lived there and would ride half way to the next line camp, meeting the other line riders and exchanging information. They were the "fences" of the open range. They would look for "sign" of cattle crossing the line or drifting. From the main ranch house "outriders" went each day to cover the range, checking the position of the cattle herds, the water supply, and grazing facilities.

Cowboys were as a rule loyal to the outfit they rode for. Their cattle, their saddle horses, and their employers were the best, and they were ready to back their opinions with their six-guns. See BARBED WIRE, CATTLE KING, OPEN RANGE.

Range Delivery. Sale of cattle on the range. The buyer had to come and get them, "sight unseen."

Ranger. See TEXAS RANGERS.

Rattlesnake. There are more than a dozen kinds of rattlesnakes, but the cowboy usually means the Texas "diamond-

back" rattler when he speaks of this reptile. In Arizona, California, and Nevada the smaller version of the rattlesnake, with a pair of horns over his eyes, is called a "sidewinder."

The Texas diamond-back has large brown or reddish diamond-shaped markings. These snakes sometimes grow to be as long as five feet, though four feet is about the average. At the tips of their tails are "buttons," or rattlers, which give off a rustling or whirring sound which can be heard

by a man at a distance of from ten to twenty yards. This is the rattler's warning—as he always tries to get away from a man or animal. But if pressed, he will coil and strike. One cowboy expert said a rattler could strike in one-tenth of a second. The farthest a rattler can strike is two-thirds of its length. The rattlesnake grows a new button every time he sheds his skin, and he does this several times a year.

The rattlesnake has many enemies who go out of their way to kill him. These include the road runner, the antelope, the peccary or wild pig, the king snake and the black snake, and the squinch owl.

Someone has said you can always tell a cowboy by the way he sits down—he always carefully examines the ground around to be sure no rattlers are near. When he has to sleep on the ground he often will place a horsehair rope around him, believing that a rattler will not cross over the bristling hairs. When he awakes in the morning he always remains very still for a moment to be sure no rattlers are in his blankets or on his chest. Snakes will not strike in the cool of the morning, and only crawl in with a cowboy to keep warm, but if the cowboy sees one on his chest he "shucks" himself of his blanket by sliding out quickly.

Some authorities claim that the death-dealing qualities of the rattlesnake have been greatly overrated, other than the black-tailed rattler of Florida. While there are few cases reported of a cowboy's dying from a rattler's bite, he always takes heroic measures to avoid the danger.

An old cowboy remedy for rattlesnake bite was: "All the booze you can drink—and a poultice over the bite made from kerosene and sliced onions. Renew when the onions turn black. Burning out with a red-hot iron is good. So is a razor or sharp knife. Cut out around the bite and suck the wound." However, cowboys learned to use whiskey sparingly as "all you can drink" acted on the heart in the same way as the rattlesnake poison—as a depressant.

In Mexico there is a small variety of the sneezewort with ash-colored leaves, known as *cebadilla*. The juice from the leaves of this plant contains a strong alkaloid, which will offset the rattlesnake poison. See BLACK SNAKE, HORSEHAIR ROPE, KING SNAKE, MEDICINE, PECCARY, PRAIRIE DOG, ROAD RUNNER, SQUINCH OWL.

Rawhide. The dried skin or hide of a deer, cow, or other animal. Rawhide was one of the most necessary materials on the Plains and has been variously termed "Mexican iron" and "Indian iron." It was used for covering the cowboy's saddle-tree. It was cut into strings and braided into hobbles, bosals, reatas, halters, and bridle reins, and, after softening, used for saddle strings.

With the hair left on, it was used for chair seats. Green rawhide strings were employed in lashing together the fence of the corral,

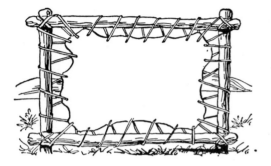

and when they dried they were like iron. Rawhide took the place of nails, hinges, and other fastenings on the ranch.

The preparation of rawhide is simple. The skin of a calf or hide of a cow when taken fresh from the animal is anchored in a stream of water, or submerged in a pool, for three or four days. It is then placed over a log or other round, smooth object and the hair "slipped off" with the back of a knife or a smoothed file. If the hair does not slip off easily, some wood ashes are sprinkled on to give the knife blade a better hold. The flesh side is next trimmed of pieces of flesh and the hide is nailed to the side of a building or placed in a frame, always in the shade. In several days it is dry and is ready for use. It can be worked easily after being soaked in water. Strings are cut from a large circle or disk of the hide. Buckskin is made from rawhide of the deer. See Buckskin, Leather, Pannier, Parfleche, Rope, Saddle, String.

Rawhides. A term applied by northern cowboys to Texans because of their habit of using rawhide to repair everything from broken bridles to wagon tongues.

Rawhiding. Joshing, or as we say today, "kidding." Sometimes rawhiding meant to torment, or abuse, or as the cowboy said, "to ride." Rawhiding might also mean whipping.

Razorbacks. Wild hogs descended from the early domesticated animals brought over by the Spanish conquerors. They thrive in the marshes of the Southwest and live on rattlesnakes, prickly pears, and acorns (mast crops). The razorback is spotted, long-snouted, long-tailed, long-bodied, and sometimes grows long tusks. These hogs were captured by the western pioneers and again domesticated. They provided the cowboy with his bacon, which he called "sow belly," "dog," or if salted, "salty

dog." The razorback is not to be confused with the American wild pig, the peccary, or javelina. See Mast Crop, Peccary.

Reata (ray-ah'ta). A rope made from braided rawhide. See Rope.

Reins. Leather or rawhide lines which are attached to the bit of the bridle and by which the rider guides and manages his mount. There are two types of reins, "open reins" and "closed reins." The Texan usually used the open reins in the old days. These were not tied together at the saddle-end, and if the rider was thrown he was in no danger of becoming entangled in them. Also, if a horse was grazing with his bridle on, he would not catch the reins in the brush. The California buckaroo favored the closed reins, which had a flexible whip, or romal, attached at the saddle-end.

When the old-time cowboy dismounted, he threw the reins over his horse's head or dropped them so that they hung to the ground. The horse could graze, but if he tried to run away he would step on the ends of the open reins, or the romal of the closed reins, and stop himself. Whenever reins were thrown loosely around a tree limb or the bar of a hitching rack, the horse considered himself tied and would not move. When a rider was prepared to mount, he was careful not to bring the reins over the horse's head until he was ready for the animal to start, for this was the signal to go for the horse.

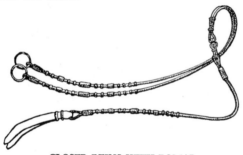

CLOSED REINS WITH ROMAL

Reins are made from straps or braided from rawhide strings or leather thongs. Some fancy reins are made from braided silver wire. Usually the reins are attached to the bit by small chains. This keeps the horse from chewing them and also adds the necessary weight to balance the Spanish and Mexican bits. Leaden weights are sometimes scattered along the lower ends of the reins and covered with braided rawhide or leather buttons, both for decoration and to balance the bit. See BIT, BRIDLE, LEATHER, ROMAL.

Remington, Frederic. Painter, sculptor, and writer, Remington was best known for his paintings of western scenes. Horses,

Indians, and soldiers were his specialty. He was born in Canton, N. Y., October 4, 1861. At the age of nineteen he went West. He wandered through the Dakotas, Montana, Kansas, and the Indian Territory, meeting and traveling with Indians, cowboys, and soldiers. He bought a ranch near Kansas City, but when this proved unsuccessful he sold out and traveled through the Southwest. His sketches of western life began to appear in *Harper's Weekly*, and he was soon illustrating books as well as magazine articles. While chiefly known as a painter, Remington also modeled statuettes of Indians, cowboys, and trappers which are full of character. He wrote and illustrated several volumes of stories, including *Pony Tracks, Crooked Trails,* and *Sundown Leflare.* He died in 1909.

Remuda (ray-moo′dah). A string of extra horses to be used as remounts. It comes from the Spanish term, *remuda de caballos,* meaning a relay of horses. During the roundup or while on the trail a cowboy had to change horses frequently. All saddle horses were pooled in one band and watched over by a wrangler. See WRANGLER.

Rep. A term used by the cowboy for "representative," or a man who came from another ranch during a roundup to sort out animals belonging to his employer. His work was called "repping," and sometimes cowboys termed him a "stray man."

Ride a Slick Saddle. To ride a saddle that does not have a saddle roll. Also called "slick riding."

Riding Fence. Riding along a line of fence on a ranch, looking for breaks or loose places in the wire. The cowboy carries a repair kit of pliers, wire and the like. Riding fence is one of the "ornery jobs" which became part of the cowboy's work after the disappearance of the open range and the coming of barbed wire. See BARBED WIRE.

Riding Herd. Driving a herd of cattle up the trail or at a roundup. See CATTLE TRAILS, ROUNDUP.

Riding Sign. The cowboy's term for following the trail of an animal or a man by "sign." The early cowboys usually had to trail lost horses or cattle, but there were times when they "rode sign" on bad men and hostile Indians. Riding sign was an art, and amounted to nothing more nor less than good detective work. Scouts called this work "trailing" or "following sign." Old markings were "old sign" and meant a cold trail, and "fresh sign" meant a hot trail.

The expert sign rider worked on the theory that no two people or two animals would leave tracks or markings exactly

alike. A worn heel or a seam in the sole of a boot would make a certain man's trail easy to follow. A chip off an animal's hoof, or a broken shoe on a horse, would help the cowboy keep on the trail of that beast. A moccasin track would tell what tribe an Indian belonged to. If a man was running, only the ball of his foot touched the ground. If he tried to throw off his trailer by walking backwards, his steps would be shorter. If he was carrying anything heavy, his heel marks would be deeper. By the position of a horse's hoofprints the cowboy could tell whether the animal was walking, trotting, or loping. When a horse had a rider on his back his hoofprints went along a regular course. If he was not being ridden he would wander around. Where there was grass, the cowboy could tell by the way it was pressed down the direction the fugitive had taken.

Nothing escaped the notice of the good sign rider. He could tell what direction a fugitive was taking by the tracks of wild animals which had been frightened out of his path. If the person being chased was going through a woods, the way the wild birds flew up would point his way. The sign rider used his eyes, his ears, his nose, and even his fingers. Every broken stick or disturbed rock or mark on the hard ground meant something to him. He had to use his brain, too, and never forget that a man being pursued would always try to back track, or wade up or down a stream of water to conceal his trail, usually coming out on the same side that he entered the stream.

After following sign for a while, the trailer might be able to figure out where the other was headed and thus take a short cut and head him off. In some thickly wooded sections a trail might suddenly end at the foot of a tree. The trailer would find that the fugitive had climbed the tree and continued on his way among the treetops by swinging from limb to limb. See SIGN.

Rifle. A firearm shot from the shoulder position and having a rifled barrel, or one with spiral grooves inside the bore, which causes the bullet to rotate or spin. A musket

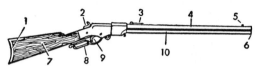

1. BUTT
2. HAMMER
3. REAR SIGHT
4. BARREL
5. FORESIGHT
6. MUZZLE
7. STOCK
8. LEVER AND TRIGGER GUARD
9. TRIGGER
10. MAGAZINE

has a smooth bore. The rifle of the old-time cowboy was commonly the shorter type, known as "carbine," but he called it a rifle. After the seventies, he usually called his rifle a Winchester, no matter what the make. He never called a rifle a "gun," as gun meant pistol, but he did call an extra-big calibered rifle a "buffalo gun." The rifle was carried in an open-mouthed scabbard slung on the left side of the saddle, with the butt of the rifle forward and the end of the scabbard passing through the leaves of the stirrup leathers.

There were many famous rifles in the early days. The single-shot Sharps used the most powerful black-powder cartridge, and was deadly up to and including 1,000 yards. The Remington single-shot rolling block rifle of .58 caliber was a famous buffalo gun. The eight-shot lever-action Spencer also was a popular rifle. The Henry .44 caliber 15-shot repeating rifle had a barrel with eight sides and was called an "8-square."

Oliver Winchester later developed the Model 73 Winchester, a repeating rifle which used a center-fire cartridge. This became the cowboy's favorite rifle, as the ammunition of the .44 caliber Winchester also fitted his .44 caliber Colt pistol. See BUFFALO GUN, CARBINE, CARTRIDGE, COLT, SHOTGUN, WINCHESTER.

Rigging. That part of the saddle which holds it secure on the horse's back, consisting of latigo, cincha or girth, and rigging rings.

There are two general types of rigging. The old-time cowboy who tied his lariat to his saddle horn and who was known as a "tie-man" used a double rig or "rim-fire rig," with two cinchas to hold his saddle securely when roping. One cincha went around the horse's belly just behind the front legs and the second one was about a foot farther back. The Californians, or buckaroos, used a single broad cincha and called it the "California rig" or "center-fire rig." The buckaroo was a "dally man" and there was not so much strain on his saddle in roping as upon that of the "tie man."

From these two basic types of rigging others have developed to suit the taste of the individual cowboy. When the single cincha is advanced to a certain point it is called a "three-quarters rig." When a horse has a sloping chest, the cinchas of the double rig are crossed beneath so as to obtain a better grip. A "light rider" uses a center-fire rig, while a "heavy rider" might require the double or rim-fire rig.

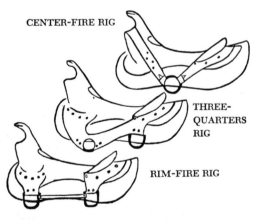

CENTER-FIRE RIG

THREE-QUARTERS RIG

RIM-FIRE RIG

When using the double rig the cowboy always tightens the forward cincha first. This is because some smart horses will swell up when the cincha is tightened and they can do this more efficiently if the rear cincha is tightened first. See CINCHA, DALLY, RIGGING RING, SADDLE, TIE-MAN.

Rigging Ring. A metal ring attached on each side of the saddle. The latigo is fastened to this ring, and, when passed through the ring on the end of the cincha and knotted, holds the cincha in position. See CINCHA, LATIGO, RIGGING, SADDLE.

Ring Bit. A bit which has a large metal ring attached at the top of the port on the

crossbar or mouth of the bit. The ring goes under the lower part of the horse's jaw. This is one of the oldest forms of bits and came over with the Spanish *conquistadores.* It was then called the "Mameluke bit." Mexicans still use it. See BIT.

Ring Spearing. Spearing a suspended metal ring with a spear or lance while riding at full speed on a horse. This ancient tourney, said to have been a sport of the Arabs, has been revived in the West during the past few years. In the early days it was a favorite sport of cowboys. The standards are upright posts with long crossarms from which the rings are suspended from cords and held by spring clips so they will come off easily on the spear. The standards, of which there are three, are spaced 33⅓ yards apart with a run of 33⅓ yards from the starting point to the first ring. The rings are about seven feet from the ground, or at about the shoulder height of the average rider. Four horsemen compose a team and the total number of rings caught determines the winning team. The rings must be on the spear after the course is completed. Rings are about two inches in diameter and spears about seven feet long.

Ringy. A term meaning mad or angry. The cowboy would say, "He's plumb ringy."

Road Agent's Spin. A tricky half-turn given to a six-gun. When the bad man was told to surrender his gun, butt first, he would keep his forefinger in the trigger guard, with the barrel down and held with the other fingers. By jerking up the butt of the gun it fell into his palm with the barrel pointing at the arresting officer. After the marshal of Tombstone was killed by one Curly Bill in this manner, it became the custom to order bad men to drop their weapons on the ground and step back from them. See PISTOL, QUICK-DRAW.

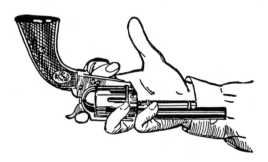

Road Brand. This was the light brand placed on cattle sufficient to "last up the trail," or to the shipping point. It was used when cattle of different brands were in the trail herd. See BRAND, CATTLE DRIVE.

Road Runner. This interesting little bird is also called *paisano* (pay-sah'no),

or "fellow countryman" along the Border, and "chaparral cock" in the North. It has short wings, but does not fly. It spreads its

wings and runs very fast along the ground. The road runner will take time off from its meals to kill a rattlesnake. As it runs toward the snake it catches up a mouthful of chaparral thorns, and weaving in and out as the snake strikes, stuffs the thorns into the reptile's mouth. It then pecks out the rattler's eyes. This is the state bird of New Mexico. See RATTLESNAKE.

Roan. A horse whose color is bay, sorrel, or chestnut, mixed with gray or white. Roan horses come in various shades, including dark blue roan, light strawberry roan, and red roan.

Rodeo (roh-day'oh). A contest where cowboys try to outdo each other in riding, roping, and other Western events. *Rodeo* is Spanish for roundup. In some sections of this country it is pronounced "roh'dee-o." The rodeo as a contest of skill grew out of the competitions cowboys held among themselves after the rodeo or roundup was over, much as the cowboys or *vaqueros* of Mexico did in their *jaripeos* (hahr-ee-pay'-ohs).

There are many exciting events in the rodeo, from the opening parade through the regular events, which include saddle bronc riding, bareback bronc riding, bull-dogging, calf roping, steer roping, bull rid-

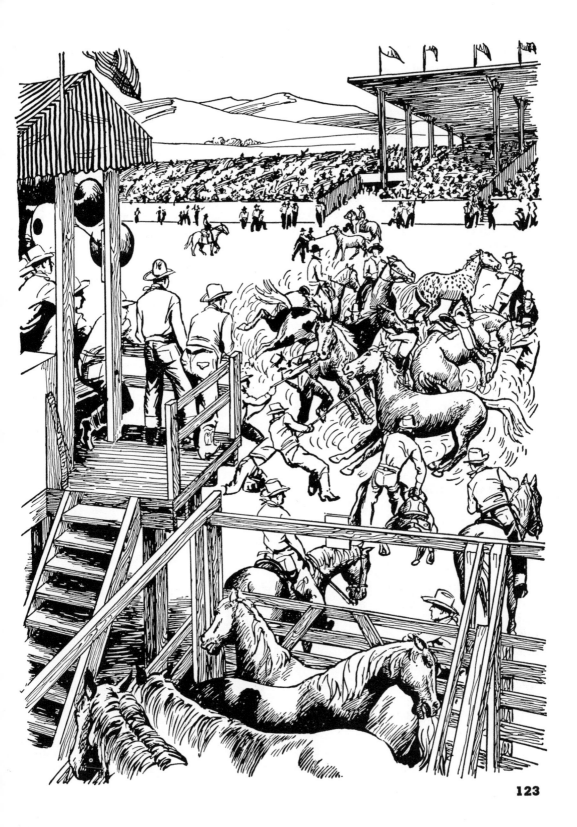

ing, team roping, wild-cow milking contests, trick riding and trick roping, the clowns, and the trained horse acts.

In the rodeo cowboys and cowgirls do many of the things that are common practice on the ranch as a part of the day's work. Saddle bronc riding is one of these, and usually is one of the most exciting events at the rodeo. The horses in saddle bronc riding, as well as those in bareback bronc riding, are untamed. They are picked for their bucking ability and many of them are what the cowboy calls "killers" and "outlaws." A bucking strap is used to make them buck, too.

The bronc is ridden with the standard Association Saddle, and without a bit. Only one rein is used. The cowboy must hold this rein six inches high in his left hand while his right hand must be lifted in the air at all times. If he touches the saddle or horse with either hand he is disqualified. To show that he is not trying to hang on with his spurs, he must rake the horse from the shoulders to the girth on the first five bucks and from the hips to the girth on the second five. When the horse stops bucking, and if the rider is still aboard, a "hazer" rides up and helps the cowboy off onto his horse or to the ground. The contest is usually about even, as the horse wins as often as the cowboy.

Bulldogging is another stirring event. The cowboy rides alongside the bull, leaps from his horse, grabs the bull by the horns, and tries to throw him. The limit for doing this is three minutes. Many bulldoggers throw the bull in less than ten seconds. In calf roping the rider must rope his calf, leap from his horse and tie the calf up with piggin' strings. He must not "bust" the calf, but if the calf runs against the rope and "busts" itself this is permitted.

In wild-cow milking, cowboys work in teams, one trying to hold the cow while the other tries to milk her. In bareback bronc riding and bull riding the rider is allowed to hold onto a surcingle (a broad strap going around the animal's body) with both hands. Even then it is a gamble whether he can stay on. The "cutting horse" contest, in which the smart little cow horses show their ability to cut steers and calves from a herd, is a favorite with Westerners.

While there are several communities which claim to have been the first to hold a rodeo, the fact is the rodeo "just growed," and it is impossible to tell where it first started in this country. Today the International Rodeo Association (IRA) makes standard rules and regulations for such contests, and is the recognized managers' association.

The rodeo cowboys themselves formed the Cowboys Turtle Association (CTA) in 1936. In 1945 this became known as the Rodeo Cowboys Association. These cowboys take part only in contests approved by their organization, lend money to members for doctors and hospital bills, and have death benefits. The amateurs also have an association known as the Cowboys Association of America which was organized "to give the beginning rodeo cowboy a chance to get started in rodeos and competition with his own class and without having to buck the top professional cowboy." When a member of the amateur association wins $2,000 in prize money in one season he is barred as an amateur and must join the Rodeo Cowboys Association.

The rodeo also has become a high school and college sport in Texas and is now as popular as football and baseball. In the last few years the rodeo has grown to be one of the biggest forms of entertainment in America. There are more than 1,000 shows in the United States and Canada every season. One writer on the rodeo showed that while 86,288 persons saw the fifth game of the World Series in 1948, more than 100,000 attended a one-day rodeo at Los Angeles. Of one hundred rodeos listed in one issue of a rodeo magazine for 1950 the total prize money was $381,150. See ASSOCIATION SADDLE, BRAHMA BULL, BUCKING, BUCKING STRAP, BULLDOGGING.

Roll. A covered cord, or welt, which sticks out a third of an inch or more from the front of the cantle on a saddle. This aids in keeping the rider from slipping back and out of his saddle when roping or riding a bucking horse. See SADDLE.

Roll His Tail. A term applied to a cow when it starts to stampede or run. The tail is humped up at the thick end and the cowboy recognizes this as a sure sign that the cow "means to go places." See STAMPEDE.

Rolling. Twirling a single-action six-gun on the forefinger. The gun is held by the butt with the finger in the trigger guard. The butt is released with a downward jerk of the muzzle and spins around on the finger. As it comes back into position the

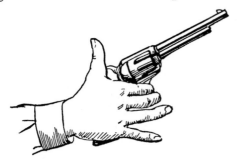

thumb catches the hammer and the gun is cocked by its own weight. This is the opposite of the "road agent's spin." See ROAD AGENT'S SPIN, PISTOL.

Roll Up. This is the roll-over a horse does when his saddle is removed. A cow-

boy, after removing the saddle, will stand and watch to be sure that his horse rolls completely over on his back three times. A horse that cannot do this is considered no good.

Romal (roh-mahl'). A long quirt or whip attached to the end of closed reins. The romal has no stiffening in the handle, and with the lash usually measures about four feet in length. See REINS.

Rope. A thick cord made of twisted fibers of hemp, flax, or other vegetable material, or from braided rawhide strings. The rope is one of the most important parts of the cowboy's gear, and in the old days he used it not only to lasso domestic animals but wild ones as well, and for many other purposes. The early cowboy was as helpless without his rope as a hunter without a gun. In the old days an excellent cowboy in the Southwest was called *uno buena reata*, literally Mexican for "a good rope."

The Texan calls his rope just that—a "rope." In the North the term "lariat" was more commonly used in former days, a term derived from *la reata* (lah ray-ah'-tah), but meaning for the northern cowboy a rope of twisted fibers. However, in the Southwest "lariat" meant a short stake rope. The cowboy also called his fiber rope a "hard twist," "whale line," "lass rope," "catch rope," or "throw rope." The early cowboy did not, call a rope a "lasso." Lasso was a verb. He "lassoed" with his rope.

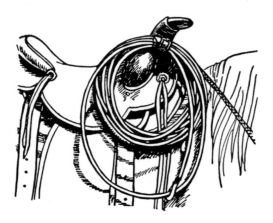

Fiber ropes come in various sizes, from three-eighths of an inch to one-half an inch in diameter. The smaller ones are used for roping calves and the larger for roping steers and horses. Fiber catch ropes vary from thirty-five to fifty feet in length. One of the best of the fiber ropes is a four-strand rope handmade by Mexicans from the maguey or aloe leaf. It has a hard, smooth finish. It is sometimes called "Peter Magay" by cowboys from the Mexican term *pita maguey* (pee'tah mah-gway'ee) for the aloe. The manila rope is made from fibers of a plant related to the banana family and is one of the best all-round ropes.

The reata, which is often termed "riata," is a rope made from four to eight braided strings or "whangs" of rawhide. This is a rope that cowboys can and do make for themselves. The newly made reata is stiff and must be softened, which is done by soaking it in warm tallow or other animal oil, then placing it around a smooth post and pulling it back and forth until it is pliable.

The rawhide reata was once employed by southwestern cowboys, but they later discarded it for the "hard twist" or fiber rope. The California buckaroos, however, never gave it up. The buckaroo's reata is about three-eighths of an inch in diameter and sixty or more feet in length. The reata requires special care, for if one of the braided strings becomes damaged the rope is worthless. Cowboys accustomed to the "hard twist" find the reata awkward. Reatas are still made but are now used more for show, hanging from the horn of a fancy saddle, than for practical roping. See BITTER END, ROPING.

Rope Horse. A horse or pony used for roping cattle. He is trained to run true behind the cow that is being chased until the noose of the lariat is thrown. He then veers off to a proper angle and props himself or "jumps into a set," to take the shock of impact off the rope. He stands firmly, holding the rope tight until his rider leaps off and ties up the cow. See CUTTING HORSE, HORSE, QUICK STOP, ROPING.

Rope Spinning. The art of twirling or spinning a rope with the noose open.

The art of spinning a rope is much in the rope itself. An ordinary rope cannot be used. The best kind is a braided sash cord, preferably what is known as "spot cord," Number 12. The rope should be about twenty feet long, although fourteen feet is long enough for the beginner. The honda, or eye-loop, is made by bending an end of the rope back upon its own part and wiring it together. The eye-loop should be about two inches on the inside.

The spin known as the "flat loop" is the simplest and easiest. The rope is opened into a large noose, held in front of the body so the lower part of the noose rests on the ground. It is then spun by making a wide circle with both loop and stem. As the loop or noose opens it is released and kept turning by holding the stem only and moving the hand in little circles from the wrist. The spoke or stem should not press against the eye-loop, but should incline toward that part of the eye-loop where it is fastened.

The flat loop is the simplest of those forms of rope spinning, known as the "flat spins," where the spinner always stands outside the loop. In another form of the flat spins, the spinner stands inside the loop. The simplest of these spins is the "wedding ring."

The second general type of rope spinning is known as the "vertical spins," where the loop is spun so that it is perpendicular to the floor. In the "skip," sometimes called the greatest of all rope-spinning tricks, the spinner jumps forward and backward through the spinning loop.

Also coming under the head of rope spinning are the trick knots which a spinner makes in his rope by a skillful twist of his wrist. These knots include the "pretzel,"

"figure-of-eight," and the "slip knot." See Roping.

Roping.   Throwing a rope or lariat so that the noose catches an animal, usually around the head, neck, or feet. Roping or lassoing is an ancient custom. However, at the time the Moors invaded Spain the method of roping was different from that used today. The roper placed the noose of his rope on the end of a ten foot pole, and riding up to the animal to be roped, placed it over that animal's head. The other end of the rope, instead of being attached to a saddle horn, was secured to the tail of the horse. The type of roping in common

HORSEBACK ROPING

use today is the adaptation of the former method by the early Mexicans.

There are two types of roping: one used when the roper is mounted and the other when he is afoot. On horseback the rope is carried in a coil on the right-hand side of the saddle. In lassoing the rider lifts the coil in his left hand, separating the honda end with his right hand. The honda end is next twirled out in a series of short jerks to make a large loop, from six to seven feet in diameter. With the palm of the right hand down and the hand grasping the loop about two feet from the honda, holding both the side of the loop and that part of the rope not yet passed through the honda, the roper shakes out his loop and begins

127

twirling it above his head in a clockwise direction. The rope is twirled until the throw is made. As soon as the rope is released that portion in the left hand is allowed to play out.

The roper's horse, when the rope is thrown, veers diagonally to the side away from the roped animal and goes into a "set," to absorb the shock when the animal hits the other end of the rope.

Such throws as these are usually made so the loop falls over the head or horns or the neck of the animal. There are other throws by cowboys which are more expert. One such throw is known as "going over the withers." The cowboy rides along the left side of the cow and with an overhand reverse swing of his loop throws it over the cow's back and keeps it in that position until both of the cow's feet are in the loop. He then swings his horse sharply to the left. The cow's feet are jerked from beneath its body and the animal "goes plumb over."

The "sure-fire way" is to rope the cow by the horns, and instead of veering off, to keep alongside while the slack in the rope is flipped over the cow's back and around its rump just above the hocks. The horse is

OVER THE HORNS

then turned sharply to the left and the cow's head is jerked back against its right side so that the animal is yanked completely around and upside down. But these two "artistic" methods are little used today because of wear and tear on the roped animal.

The roper on foot usually does not twirl his rope over his head. He tosses the loop which is spread out on the ground alongside him or is trailing him if he is walking. This type of roping commonly takes place in a corral. One method is called "fore-footing" and the other "hind-footing."

STANDING ROPING

The *mangana* (mahn-gah'nah), or "fore-footing," can also be done on horseback, but it is usually performed when the roper is on foot. The rope is tossed in the path of the running animal and jerked when the forefeet are in the loop.

The "peal," as the cowboy terms it, from the Mexican *pialar* (pee-ahl'ar), means a catch by the hind feet. It also can be an artistic throw if performed by an expert. The rope is tossed so that the loop forms a figure 8, and one half of the loop catches one foot while the other half catches the other.

In roping on foot the cowboy gives the rope a turn about his hips and when the animal hits the other end he digs in with his high-heeled boots. He may give the rope a turn about a snubbing post if one is handy.

Roping is sometimes dangerous. If a roped animal runs toward the horse and the horse "spooks," the cowboy is liable to find himself wrapped up in the rope. If he does not free himself before the cow reaches one end and the horse the other he may suffer severe injuries. See DALLY, HONDA, LASSO, NECK ROPE, RODEO, ROPE, TIE-MAN.

Rosadero (roh-sa-day′ro). This is the part of the saddle commonly called the "fender," which is below the stirrup straps and which protects the rider's legs from rubbing against a sweating horse, and also protects the horse from the rubbing of the stirrup leathers. See SADDLE.

Rosette. A leather tie ornament used as a decoration and fastening on saddles and bridles. They have two slits through which the tie strings pass. Leather rosettes

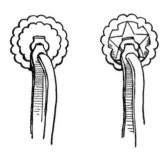

are commonly used in pairs, with a smaller one on top. See CONCHA, LEATHER BRAIDING, TIE STRINGS.

Roughing Out. The first riding of an unbroken horse. See BUST.

Roughneck. Term for dude-ranch employes such as cowboys, wranglers, cooks, packers, guides, irrigation and chore boys. They are also sometimes called "savages." See DUDE.

Rough Rider. See BRONCO BUSTER.

Rough String. Unruly horses and outlaws in a remuda. Such horses are usually given as punishment to the cowboy who mistreats horses. See OUTLAW, REMUDA.

Roundup. The herding of cattle or horses on the open range or on ranches to a central point for branding, tallying, or sorting out for shipment or other purposes. In the old days roundups were made over large sections of the open range and many ranchers took part, each sorting out his own animals.

The first roundups of cattle were known as "cowhunts." This was because the cattle in the brush country along the Border had to be driven from the dense chaparral and other thorny brush. Sometimes dogs were employed, and instead of roping the animals they were "tailed," or thrown by riding alongside them, catching hold of their tails, and turning them over. They were tied up and later driven out of the brush by tying them up with gentle oxen.

When the cattle grazed on the open plains the roundups were held twice a year. In the spring the calves and mavericks were branded, and the cattle sorted out according to ownership. In the fall another roundup was held, and the calves that had been missed in the spring were branded and the "beef herds" cut out for shipment. Roundups still are held on the bigger ranches and in Arizona, New Mexico, southern Utah, Nevada, and Montana, where many good-sized cattle outfits continue to use the public domain.

The roundup is in charge of the "roundup boss," or "captain." He groups his cowboys in pairs and they start out from camp on the "outer circle." This is not actually a circle but more like a triangle or segment of a circle. The cowboys begin driving the cows in toward camp where they are grouped and held as a herd. Those wanted for branding or other purposes are cut out and driven into the inner circle.

In the roundup the cattle are counted by "tallying"; that is, they are strung out and driven in a long line past two cowboys who count them. A "quick tally" is sometimes made by counting every calf branded as five cattle. Thus 200 branded calves would mean a herd of 1,000 cattle. The home base of the roundup is the chuckwagon. Here the cowboys eat and sleep, and from this point the roundup boss starts them out on circle each morning. Most cattle today are driven into corrals when rounded up. See CHUCK WAGON, CIRCLE RIDER, COW HUNT, DOG, LONGHORNS, MAVERICK, OPEN RANGE, TAIL, TALLY.

Run. A fast gallop. See GAIT.

Running Iron. See BRANDS, BRANDING IRON, RUSTLER.

Running Mount. See PONY-EXPRESS MOUNT.

Russell, Charles Marion. A painter, writer, and sculptor. Russell has been called

both "the cowboy artist," and the "cowboy's artist." Will Rogers once said of him, "He is the only painter of western pictures that the cowpuncher can't criticize. Every little piece of leather or rope is just where it should be." Russell loved the West, and lived there during that period when the open range and the buffalo were disappearing, the great roundup days were passing, and the Indians were being herded into reservations.

He was born March 19, 1864, at Oak Hill, a suburb of St. Louis, Missouri. As a youth he went West at the age of sixteen and worked for years with various cattle outfits in the Territory of Montana. His first pictures of cowboy life were sold "across the mahogany" in saloons. Later he illustrated books, among them Emerson Hough's *The Story of the Cowboy;* wrote and sketched for magazines and publishing houses, notably for *The Outing* and *Scribner's;* and exhibited in New York, Los Angeles, Chicago, Minneapolis, Denver, Calgary, Winnipeg, Manitou, and London.

Among his better-known paintings are "Where the Great Herds Drink," "Trail's End," and "Waiting for a Chinook." One of his best was a buffalo hunt, "When Meat Was Plenty," owned by Will Rogers. His largest painting, "Lewis and Clark at Ross' Hole," is in the House of Representatives at Helena, Montana. His statues include "Bucker and Buckaroo," "Spirit of Winter," "Where the Best Riders Quit," and "Changing Outfits." Many statuettes were modeled in semi-permanent composition. His horses were in different "walking positions," and he used the models to sketch from when planning a picture. Some models later were cast in bronze. He wrote many books and stories, including the famous "Rawhide Rawlins" stories. It was his habit when writing letters to decorate them with lively sketches of western scenes. He was a friend and adviser of many young western artists, including Will James and Joe De Yong. Russell died October 2, 1926, at Great Falls, Montana.

Rusties. Undeveloped cattle or "sorry little dogies," which were cut out before the herd started up the trail.

Rustle. When applied to cattle and horses, "to rustle" meant to steal. If applied to anything else the word had no unfavorable meaning. A cowboy might "rustle" a meal, which meant just going and getting one.

doing wrong so long as they did not hurt any real Westerners. Another type of rustler thought that both cows and the range were free. They rustled cattle because they were "plumb sentimental about cows" — just couldn't resist them. But they spared those belonging to widows, orphans, and the poor.

The worst type of rustler, the type portrayed in novels, in the movies, and in tele-

Rustler. A horse or cattle thief. Cattle rustlers were divided into several types. There were those men who went out and picked up what they called "a few ownerless animals," mostly unbranded strays and mavericks. Then there was a class of rustler who went a little further and took a few cows from large herds owned by Easterners or foreigners. They did not feel they were

vision westerns, was the professional rustler. He made a business of stealing. The professional rustler did exist in the old West and so did the other types. Many a cowboy got his start as a cattleman by a "little innocent rustling," and many another became the main figure at a vigilance committee "necktie party" because of rustling which was not so innocent.

Rustlers were also called "sticky loopers," "long ropers," and "hoodoos." See Bad Man, Blotching, Brands, Horse Stealing, Maverick, Rustler War, Sleeper, Waddie.

Rustler War. An uprising in Johnson County, Wyoming, during 1891-92, between members of the Cattlemen's Association and cattle rustlers. These cattle rustlers, for the most part, were not professional cattle thieves but were farmers and homesteaders who were stealing from large cattle companies.

The Wyoming Rustler War, which also was known as the "Johnson County Raid," came as a climax to the ill-feeling which had been general throughout the cattle country between the nester and the rancher. There had been some pilfering of cattle, mainly unbranded calves, from the great herds which could be laid to the nesters. Then when the Burlington Railroad's western extension pushed into Wyoming, many found it profitable to supply railroad workmen with beef, as the buffalo hunters had formerly supplied such workers with buffalo meat. Cattle were stolen from the large herds to supply this beef, and the rustlers were in many cases nesters. This type of rustler was known as a "waddie."

Another cause of friction had arisen in the county. The nesters had become so numerous that they held all public offices and their ill-feeling against the cattlemen was shown in the courts when professional rustlers were brought up for trial. During four years previous to the outbreak there had been 108 indictments for cattle stealing and only one conviction, this in a case where the charge had been reduced to petty larceny.

The cattlemen, feeling they could obtain no justice in the courts and seeing their herds diminishing, decided to take the law into their own hands. They employed detectives who learned of the activities of the rustlers, and many of the latter were hanged by vigilance committees. A group of fifty Texas bad men was imported into Johnson County by the cattlemen and a general war started. This was finally stopped by the United States Cavalry, after a dozen men had been killed.

This war was what might be termed the "showdown," and when it was over, the homesteader was in the West to stay and the days of the open range were gone forever. The influence of this conflict was felt throughout the entire West.

The result of the war was that many great cattle interests sold out, and the honest settlers who had previously aligned themselves with thieves for protection against the big cattle interests now elected and supported officials who put an end to cattle rustling. See Rustler.

Saddle. A seat of leather with a high horn and cantle, secured to a horse's back to support a rider. The cowboy's saddle is designed primarily for work. It has been termed his workbench. Fashioned, in a way, after the Arabian type of saddle ridden by the Spanish conquerors, it has been further developed by the cow trade, and is like no other saddle in the world.

The saddle is the first, last, and most important piece of equipment of the cowboy. It may cost from $50 to $1,000, but once the cowboy gets the saddle he wants he will not part with it except in case of dire necessity. He will sell his horse and almost anything else he owns, but he will keep his saddle. A man without a saddle is no longer a cowboy.

The cowboy's saddle is heavy, weighing from thirty to forty pounds. It has to be heavy because of the nature of his work, for a lighter saddle would be torn to pieces in roping steers and horses. The high cantle, or back of the seat, gives the rider a firm seat in roping or riding a raw bronc. The high pommel or horn is steel forged and covered with rawhide and leather. It serves to anchor the rope or lariat.

The "tree" of the saddle, made from hardwood and covered with rawhide, is forked in such a fashion that it rests snugly over the horse's back. The saddle is held on the horse with one or two broad girths or cinchas which make saddle and horse "practically one fabric." The long and heavy wooden or metal stirrup is to protect a rider's foot from being crushed should the horse fall on him, or when he is riding through timber or among cattle and horses. As further protection against thorns and brush the stirrups are sometimes covered with leather shields, called "taps" or "tapaderos."

While many Mexican *vaqueros* make their own saddles, the saddle of the American cowboy is generally built by a professional manufacturer. The chief difference in saddles is usually in the tree, or foundation of the saddle. Certain differences distinguish the old California, Brazos, White River, Nelson, Oregon, and Cheyenne types, as well as many modern ones.

After the hardwood tree, with its longitudinal fork and transverse cantle and bolted-on metal horn, is covered with rawhide, it is fastened down on a curved, leathern plate which rests on the horse's back. This plate is termed the "skirt." As it

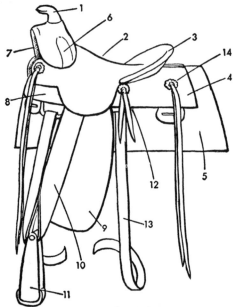

1. HORN
2. SEAT
3. CANTLE
4. BACK JOCKEY
5. SKIRT
6. SWELL
7. GULLET
8. FRONT JOCKEY
9. FENDER (ROSADERO)
10. STIRRUP LEATHER
11. STIRRUP
12. CINCHA RING
13. LATIGO
14. CONCHA AND TIE

the horse's sweat and also from chafing. These shields are called "fenders" or "rosaderos" (roh-sah-der′os). Also attached to the tree on either side and beneath the stirrup leathers are one or two rigging rings, to which the cincha or girth is fastened.

There are a series of tie-strings on either side of the saddle. These serve a double purpose. They help hold the saddle together and are used by the cowboy to tie on and carry various things like a poncho, blanket roll, or supplies.

As leather carving and saddle-stamping were once almost exclusively used in decorating saddles, most saddles are ornamented in this fashion today. Others are decorated with silver and "horse jewelry," and some saddles of the Southwest are decorated after the Mexican fashion with "chomite," or a woolen embroidery worked onto the leather. Many saddles, made by skilled craftsmen, are ornamented with leather braidwork. See CINCHA, CONCHA, DALLY, LEATHER BRAIDING, LEATHER CARVING, RIGGING, ROSETTE, SADDLE BLANKET, SADDLE STAMPING, STIRRUP, TAPADEROS.

is divided into halves it is usually spoken of as "skirts," or "bastos." These skirts are further lined with a leather "sudadero" (soo-dah-der′o), or sort of sweat band. The skirts, made of heavy oak-tanned leather, reach so far down that the saddle rests securely on the horse's back, and is hard to dislodge even when the cincha is not fastened.

On top of the skirt on either side, and fitted snugly to the horn and cantle, are two stirrup leathers, at the lower end of which are fastened the stirrups. The stirrup leathers are fastened directly to the tree. There are two broad leather shields in back of the stirrup leathers which serve to keep them from rubbing the horse's sides as well as to protect the rider's legs from

Saddle Blanket. The blanket or padding placed between the saddle and the back of the horse. The finest saddle blankets are those woven by the Navajo Indians. These blankets are made entirely by hand. The Indians raise their own sheep,

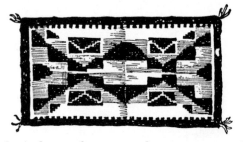

shear the wool, scour it, dye it, spin it, and weave it into rugs. They seldom make two rugs alike. The predominating colors are black and red for designs, with white or gray for the backgrounds or the bodies.

Single blankets come in sizes averaging 30 x 30 inches; double blankets range from 28 x 56 inches to 34 x 68 inches, the length being approximately twice the width. The blankets sell by the pound, and it takes from two to three and one-half pounds of material for a single blanket and four to seven pounds for a double one. Next to Navajo blankets, the best grade is the domestic woven Angora pad. See CORONA.

Saddle Pockets. Leather bags or pockets, joined together by a leathern band and hung across the saddle, usually behind the cantle. Old-time cowboys sometimes called these "cantineses," from the Spanish word *cantina* (kahn-tee'nah), meaning saddle pocket.

Saddle Stamping. A method of decorating leather with metal stamps of various designs. Saddle stamping is an ancient craft and was used by the Moors in ornamenting their leather saddles. It was introduced into Mexico at the time of the Spanish conquerors.

Though used in conjunction with leather carving, saddle stamping frequently is the sole decoration. Vegetable-tanned leather is employed. First the leather is dampened

and saddle-soaped and allowed to dry until it returns almost to its natural shade. Then the design of the stamp is impressed on the surface by striking the top of the stamp with a heavy stick or mallet. The impression becomes darker than the surface of the leather, and remains so when the leather is dry. To make it more dark or brown, the stamp is sometimes heated.

Full-flowered effects are obtained by covering the surface of the leather with stamping. A basket-weave effect is obtained by interlocking the impressions of a basket-weave stamp. Some of the common saddle stamps are known as "sunburst," "pine tree," "star," "leaf," "horseshoe," "acorn," and "rosette." Some craftsmen make their own stamps by filing down the heads of sixteen- or twenty-penny nails. See LEATHER, LEATHER CARVING.

Sagebrush. A shrubby plant found on the arid, alkaline plains regions of the West. In some cases the brush is a dwarfed shrub, and in others it grows to treelike proportions. The trunk or stem of the plant is twisted and knotty and is covered with a light gray, shreddy bark. In some places, known as "sagebrush flats," the plant grows as high as the head of a man on horseback.

Sagebrush Men. A term southwestern cowboys applied to northern cowboys, especially those of Wyoming and Montana where there is a prevalence of sagebrush.

Salt Hoss. Corned beef. See CHUCK.

Salty Dog. A man who was considered better than anyone else in his line, whether it was shooting, roping, riding, cattle rustling, holding up trains and stagecoaches, or just "plumb orneriness."

"Dog" was also one of the old-time cowboy's terms for bacon. When salty it was "salty dog."

Santa Fé Trail. The Santa Fé Trail ran from Independence, Missouri, to the village of Santa Fé, New Mexico, a distance of about 780 miles. It twisted through Kansas, the Indian Territory, Colorado, and New Mexico; across swamps, rivers, hills, plains, and mountains.

Going west from Independence the Santa Fé Trail forked just the other side of Dodge City, Kansas. One route cut south and was known as the Desert Route, and the other ran along the north bank of the Arkansas River and was called the Mountain Route. The Desert Route was shorter but was considered more dangerous as it passed through territory claimed and controlled by the Kiowas, Apaches, and Comanches. The Mountain Route was longer and was more difficult. It generally took from two to three months for a caravan to pass over the Santa Fé Trail, while a horseman could make it in about a month. Felix X. Aubrey, one of the greatest riders of the West, once covered the 780 miles in six days to win a bet of $1,000 from the scout, Kit Carson.

At Santa Fé the trail turned south over the *Jornada del Muerto* (Journey of the Dead Man) through the Great Pass of the North (El Paso) and crossed the desert at Chihuahua, Mexico.

The Santa Fé Trail was already a very old Mexican trail when Captain William Becknell opened it as a trading route in 1821. After this the trail was much used by Americans. Los Angeles lay 1,000 miles to the west of Santa Fé, but there was no trail to this Pacific coast town.

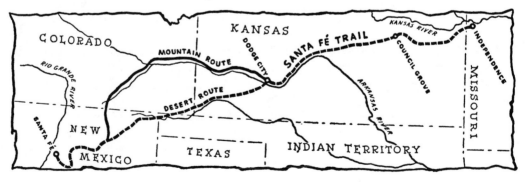

Sarape (sar-ah′pay). A type of woolen blanket or mantle made in Mexico, usually misspelled "serape" by western writers. The sarape was commonly used by old-time southwestern cowboys as a blanket at night and as a protection against cold and rain during the day. When not in use it was carried in a roll behind the cantle of the saddle. The sarape with a slit in the center through which the head passed was termed a "jorongo" (ho-rohn′go). Both styles measured about five by seven feet. The most practical type was made in Santa Ana Chiautempan, Tlaxcala, Mexico; and the more colorful ones were made in Saltillo, Mexico.

Sash. A long, wide, silken or woolen band which the southwestern cowboy of former days wore around his waist in place

of a belt. It was generally red. The cowboy took over the sash from the Mexican *vaquero,* who called his sash by the Spanish name *faja* (fah-hah).

Sashay. To go or move along, especially with a gliding or skipping step. Some say the word came from the French *chassé,* which meant to glide. It is a term much used in calling the steps of a square dance, as, "Partners join hands and sashay down the middle." The cowboy used it in connection with his horse and with people. He would say, "That hoss sashayed over the trail," or "That hombre sashayed up to me."

Savage. Term for an employe of a dude ranch. See Dude, Roughneck.

Savvy. The cowboy's way of pronouncing the Spanish word *sabe,* which means "you know" or "he knows." The cowboy used it in place of "understand." A man, too, could have "savvy," or knowledge.

Scabbard. The open-mouthed leather sheath for a rifle. A six-gun went into a holster and a knife into a sheath. See Rifle.

Scalp. An Indian custom of removing a part of the hair from the head of a fallen enemy. The practice grew out of and became necessary because of false claims made by braves in killing their enemies. With a scalp they could prove such claims. The cowboy was always alert "to keep his hair where it belonged."

Scalping was not always fatal. There are numerous cases of people who lived after being scalped. In 1867 a man was scalped in Nebraska. The Indian in mounting his horse dropped the scalp and the man got up, put the scalp in a pail of water and went to find a doctor. He recovered, and later had his scalp tanned and presented it to the Omaha Public Library. Another time, a freight conductor of the Union Pacific Railroad was scalped, two Indians helping themselves to different parts of his hair. But he lived.

The size of the scalp varied greatly. Sometimes an Indian would take a piece no larger than a silver dollar, but when scalping a man with full beard he might take all the scalp and the beard as well. In scalp dances the scalps were hung from poles. Some Indians made robes from scalps. Chief Crooked Hand at the Pawnee War Dance in 1862 had a robe made of seventy-one scalps, the scalps averaging about four inches in diameter. See Indian.

Scouts. Men who knew the lore of the plains and mountains and Indian ways, used by the United States Army as guides. The frontiersmen, trappers, and cowboys often were employed as scouts. Most of them had learned their lessons from the Indians and could travel independently of compass points or geography, depending upon landmarks such as mountains, plains, rocks and valleys, sometimes on a lone tree, the quality of the grass, or even the nature of the soil. They knew the location of obscure watering places on the prairies and the short cuts through the rough country, where they were thoroughly at home.

Among the famous scouts were Kit Carson, who guided Frémont to the West Coast; Wild Bill Hickok and Buffalo Bill Cody, who were scouts for Custer, Merritt, and Carr; James Bridger, who established Fort Bridger on the Mormon Trail; Tazewell Woody, John Yancey, Dave Rhodes, Jim Scott, Pierre Duval, and Amos Chapman. See CODY, HICKOK, RIDING SIGN.

Section. In the roomy West they spoke of "sections of land." A section is 640 acres or a square mile.

Seeing Daylight. Seeing a space between the rider and the saddle. This means a bad rider. The cowboy sits firmly, even while his horse is trotting, rather than take the easier way of posting, because he does not want any one "to see daylight."

Set Down. To order a cowboy to dismount and leave the ranch on foot, or on a borrowed horse. To be discharged or fired from a job was not considered bad by the cowboy, but to be "set down" was a disgrace. His behavior would have to be very bad to cause him to be "set down."

Sewing Horse. A stool with a large wooden clamp used by saddle-makers. The worker sits on the stool and the leather he is sewing is held in the clamp or vise.

Shack. The main ranch house. See RANCH.

Shadow Rider. A cowboy who likes to ride along and look admiringly at his shadow on the ground. Commonly applied to sporty cowboys who are vain or "stuck up."

Shavetail. A horse that has been broken to ride. The name came from the former practice of pulling some hair from the tail of a horse after he had been broken so he could be told from those not yet ridden.

Shebang. Old-time term for hide-out or meeting place of outlaws. In some parts the term also meant a house.

Sheep. The coming of sheep to the western plains helped doom the free range as a grazing land for cattle and horses. Nothing would make a cowboy madder than the mention of sheep. To be called a sheepman or a sheepherder was the lowest form of insult. The sheep made dust beds of the grassy benches; their sharp hoofs tore the grass up by the roots, after they had nibbled the grass to the ground. Their odor was said to have been disagreeable not only to cowboys but to horses and cattle.

Once they had used a water hole no cow or horse would drink from it. Many bloody battles were fought between cowboys and sheepmen. See OPEN RANGE.

Shell. A loaded shotgun shell, usually made of paper with a metal head. A "rifle shell" is not a correct expression. "Cartridge" is right for rifles, and the metal part of a cartridge is called a "case." See CARTRIDGE, SHOTGUN.

Shotgun. A smooth-bore gun made to shoot pellets or shot. This was one firearm that the early cowboy usually named correctly. He also had another name for shotgun and this was "scatter gun."

Most shotguns on the Plains were short-barreled, the barrel commonly being sawed

off. The shells were loaded with buckshot and pieces of nails, making them more deadly at close range than the rifle or pistol.

Shotguns were carried by guards on stagecoaches and by some town marshals. The 10-gauge was the usual size. One of the favorites was the Greener 10-gauge. See BUCKSHOT, GAUGE, SHELL.

Side-lining. Hobbling by tying together the front foot and hind foot on the same side of a horse, about three feet apart. When opposite feet are tied it is known as "cross hobbling." See CROSS HOBBLE, HOBBLES.

Sidewinder. A rope fastened around a horse's neck and drawn tightly along his side and tied to his tail so that he could not run away. He could walk only in a circle.

Sidewinder is also the name of a small rattlesnake. See RATTLESNAKE.

Sign. A term for something that showed a man or beast had been in a certain place. "Sign" was not a trail, but many signs could make a trail which could be followed by an expert. "Sign" might be a footprint, a broken stick, a rock moved out of place, trampled-down grass, a deserted campfire, or even the leaf of a tree found on the ground, when trees from which such a leaf came did not grow in the neighborhood. Cowboys were always on the lookout for "sign." See RIDING SIGN.

Signals. The old-time cowboy used several means of signaling. One was to fire his gun or rifle three times, the shots evenly spaced. This was a distress signal. To attract attention he would swing his hat overhead from the right to the left. If he was in sight of those he wanted to signal, he would ride his pony around in small circles. This meant to hurry up for a talk or powwow. If after riding his pony around in circles he fired his gun three times, it meant bad news. When approaching as a friend, he raised his right arm upright.

The cowboy also used Indian smoke and mirror signals. For smoke signals he built a small fire and threw some grass over it to make it smoke. Then by holding his banket over the smoke, and raising the corner, he could make long or short puffs. The meaning of a puff or a column of smoke would be decided on beforehand. Mirror signals were used in much the same way by making long and short flashes. Indians used blanket signals, waving their blankets to attract attention.

Single-Action. A one-shot, single barrel firearm—rifle, pistol, or revolver. The hammer had to be pulled back with the thumb on each shot. Instead of pulling the hammer back with the ball of his thumb, as the novice does, the experienced gunfighter pulled it with the second joint of his thumb as the hand closed around the gun in drawing. See DOUBLE-ACTION.

Sioux. See INDIAN.

Sire. A male parent horse. See DAM.

Six-Shooter. This was the name the Texas Rangers gave to the Walker Colt, named in honor of Captain Samuel H. Walker in 1846. The term "six-shooter" spread throughout the West and was used to mean any Colt revolver, or other gun that held six cartridges. See COLT, PISTOL.

Sky Pilot. The cowboy's name for a circuit rider, missionary, or preacher. The "sky pilots" of early western days were a hardy breed. The frontier towns were said to be "west of God." Ministers and other religious leaders traveled from ranch to ranch. They were always welcome, and ranchers would call in all their cowboys for religious services. In the settlements there were crude churches, and revival meetings were often held in the open air. Ministers performed marriages, christened babies, and worked hard to mend the ways and save the souls of the cowboys and Indians.

Slapping Leather. Drawing the six-gun.

Sleeper. An unbranded calf earmarked by a cattle thief who expected it to be overlooked at branding time because of the earmark. He returned later and placed his own brand on it. This was called "sleepering."

Sleeve Draw. Drawing a gun which had been concealed up the sleeve. The gun was tied to a string fastened to the galluses at the shoulder. When the hand was jerked down the gun fell into it. The .41 caliber derringer was a favorite gun for this purpose. See DERRINGER, HIDE-OUT.

Slick or **Slick Ear.** See MAVERICK.

Slicker. A raincoat made of oiled canvas, also called a "fish." The yellow slicker had many uses. It was the old-time cowboy's suitcase, and he carried his kitchen utensils, grub, and other belongings in it, rolled up and tied behind his saddle cantle. He spread it on the damp ground as his bed, and used it to cover his saddle when it was raining. It came in handy during a cattle stampede, when he waved it and slapped it in the face of the lead cattle. Wearing it himself, however, was something else. One old-timer said: "No, folks, a cowpuncher won't put on a slicker until he's darn sure the rain's plumb wet and is going to hang on for a few hours. I've seen half a dozen cowpunchers get soaked while they waited for one of the bunch to weaken and untie that water-shedder." See PONCHO.

Slick Riding. See RIDE A SLICK SADDLE.

Slopers. See WESTERNER.

Snaking. Dragging at the end of a rope, the cowboy's favorite way of "totin' things." The term "snake" also meant a bad steer.

Snubbing Post. A post set in the middle of a corral for tying up unbroken horses. It is at the snubbing post that the bronc gets his first lessons in being "gentled."

The rope which holds him is turned around the post and the horse is allowed to fight until he realizes he cannot get away. The snubbing post also was used formerly to hold animals while they were being branded. See BUST.

Sombrero (som-bray'roh). Spanish for "hat." Cowboys sometimes called their hats sombreros. See HAT, STETSON.

Son of a Gun. A term the cowboy borrowed from the men-of-war's men of the old-time sailing ships. In those days sailors' wives sometimes accompanied them on their voyages. They usually slept between the great guns, and when a son was born there he was called "son of a gun." In the West it was a term of general good-fellowship and was usually preceded by "old," as "you old son of a gun." It was not an expression which caused the cowboy to say, "Smile when you say that, stranger."

Son-of-a-Gun Stew. This was a famous cow-camp hash, or stew, usually made from kitchen scraps. See CHUCK.

Sougan (sug'gan). The comforter which a cowboy carried in his duffle bag. See DUFFLE BAG.

Spanish Gun. A cheap, cast-iron revolver made in imitation of the Colt and other western-type guns. It was dangerous and liable to blow up on firing. The only mark such guns carried was "Made in Spain," and they were made by unscrupulous manufacturers. Only tenderfoots bought them, as experienced Westerners knew their guns.

Spooky. Said of a horse that is easily frightened. He might even shy at a moving leaf or some small, unusual sound. To "spook" is to frighten.

Spread. See RANCH.

Spurs. A pointed metal implement secured to the boot of a rider, usually having a wheel or rowel with blunt-edged

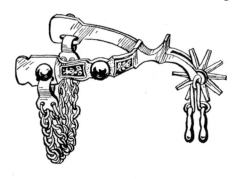

points. Spurs are a cowboy's pride and joy. One writer said the early cowboy regarded his spurs so highly that he would sooner appear in public without his pants than without his spurs.

Spurs are used chiefly to punish a horse, and when he feels the points of the rowels in his sides he knows he has done something wrong. Spurs also help a cowboy to hold on when a bronc is bucking. When

employed for this purpose the wheels or rowels are wired or tied so they cannot turn. Some spurs have a "buck hook" on the upper part of the shank which can be hooked into the cincha or girth.

The base of a spur consists of a metal heel band which goes around the upper part of the boot heel. On the two forward ends of this band are heel-band buttons, to which the spur leathers or spur straps are fastened. The two chains which pass beneath the boot and rest just forward of the boot heel also are attached to these heel-band buttons. At the back of the heel band, welded on, is the shank, and at the end of the shank is the rowel or wheel. The shank curves downward. To the pin which holds the rowels in place may be attached jingle-bobs or danglers, little pear-shaped metal ornaments which jingle when the cowboy walks or rides.

Some rowels are no larger than a twenty-five cent piece, but in the early days many were six inches or more in diameter. The points of the rowels are blunt.

If a cowboy of the old days wanted really to attract attention when off his horse, he would unfasten one of the chains which passed under his boot and let it drag. The rowel would roll along the ground or floor, the danglers would jingle, and it was calculated no fair lady could resist such sweet music. Extra-fancy spurs might be entirely of silver and sometimes were engraved in elaborate patterns.

The spur straps are carved and stamped and decorated with a silver concha. Most cowboys wear the spur-strap buckle on the inside, but some wear it on the outside. The argument as to which is right is still going on today. Spurs have always been a part of the rider's equipment and came to America on the elaborate boots of the early Spanish conquistadores. See BUCKHOOK, DANGLERS, HUNG UP,

Squaw Man. A white man married to an Indian woman. While this was a term which was sometimes applied to a man as a mark of contempt, it was not always justified. Many prominent men of the West married Indian women, notably Granville Stuart, one of the biggest cattlemen in Montana, and the author of *Forty Years on the Frontier*. When his first Indian wife died he married another. Although some white men deserted their Indian wives when white women came to the Plains country, most of them were loyal. E. C. (Teddy Blue) Abbot, also a prominent Montana rancher, who married one of Stuart's daughters, said of Indian wives, "Those Indian women made wonderful wives. The greatest attraction in a woman, to an Indian, was obedience. Their husband's will was their law. Every white man I ever knew that was married to an Indian . . . thought the world of them."[1]

Squeeze Chute. A narrow, fenced lane between two corrals into which older cattle were crowded to be branded or doctored. They were packed in so tight they could not move about. See CORRAL.

[1] From *We Pointed Them North*, by E. C. Abbot, *op. cit.*

Squinch Owl. The old-time cowboy's name for the burrowing owl. This small owl usually lived in prairie-dog holes. The

Indians called it the "dancing owl" because of its habit of dancing up and down. The squinch owl could, and would, kill a rattlesnake. See PRAIRIE DOG, RATTLESNAKE.

Stagecoach. The old western stagecoach, floating on leather bands that allowed it to pitch like a canoe in rough water, is today a symbol of the old-time West. It was rough riding in these old Concord stages. Long leather braces took the place of springs. The body of the coach was rounding and fitted snugly on those leather bands, which were about three inches wide and of four to six layers of heavy leather. Often the passengers were badly mixed up on rough roads and got sore heads from striking the roof. When the coach was full (six passengers), they could wedge together and hold to the sides, but when there were only two or three, somebody usually got hurt. The stage rocked forward and back, but not so much from side to side. The driver and guard climbed into what was called the "boot," on or at the bottom of which lay the express box. The boot seat was divided by an iron stanchion, and heavy leather belts were buckled across the men's waists, otherwise they could not stay on. Concord and Thoroughbrace stages were the same; they had thick tires about two and one-half inches wide and wooden hubs, but they were sure some hubs. The driver drew $150 a month and the guard four dollars a day and expenses.

The stagecoaches were drawn by four or six horses. The old type coach went out when steel springs were invented. See JERKY, OVERLAND STAGE.

Staked Plains (Llano Estacado). The name of a vast tableland in western Texas and eastern New Mexico which measures 150 miles east and west and 400 miles north and south. It is a part of the Great Plains and a continuation of the high plains region of Texas, bounded by the Canadian River on the north, the Pecos River on the west, and the headwaters of the Red, Brazos, and Colorado rivers on the east. The Texas Panhandle is today a part of the old Staked Plains, which the Mexicans called *Llano Estacado* (lyah'no es-tah-cah'do).

There was plenty of buffalo grass on the Staked Plains, and buffaloes in going back and forth from north and south passed through this section at certain seasons. It was a favorite hunting ground for the Plains Indians. See BUFFALO.

Stake Rope. A Texas term for a picket rope or rope for tying up a horse.

Stampede. A wild running away of animals, due to fright. This was the cowboy's nightmare. At night the slightest unusual sound or movement might start a stampede of cattle on the trail. They were especially nervous and restless during a storm, and a crack of thunder or a flash of lightning might terrorize them. Cowboys

rode around the herd singing and whistling to keep the cattle calm. They did not dare strike a match to light a cigarette. On quiet nights even the sound of a pony shaking a saddle might start the herd off.

A herd of several thousand cattle on a stampede, thundering blindly through and over everything in their path, was a terrible sight. In a stampede the cowboy's idea was to turn back the lead cattle and get the herd to milling around to tire the cattle out. They tried to turn back the lead cattle by waving their slickers, shouting, and even sometimes shooting them. Many a rider lost his life when his pony stumbled and fell in front of a stampeding herd.

Horses stampeded, too, and were harder to round up. Stampeding a band of horses was the favorite method of the Indians when on horse-stealing raids.

The word "stampede" comes from the Spanish *estampida* (es-tahm-pee'dah), meaning a crash or loud noise. See BUFFALO, CATTLE DRIVE, CORRAL, COWBOY SONGS, NIGHT HERDING, ROLL HIS TAIL.

Steer. A cowboy explained a steer once as a "male cow who had been operated on so he could never be a family man." The cowboy seldom used the term "steer." If a herd was made up of steers he called it a "beef herd." If it was steers and cows together he called it a "cow herd." See CATTLE.

Stetson. The cowboy term for hat. The original Stetson hat was made in Philadelphia by John B. Stetson. Stetson, a sickly youth, had made his first hat on an expedition to Pike's Peak in 1863, when he realized the need of some kind of protection against the rain, snow, and sun of the Plains country. This hat was fashioned with crude tools, including a hatchet. Felt material was made in those days by scrap-

ing the fur from the dried skins of rabbits, chewing it up, and spitting the juice through the teeth. Stetson employed this old-time method and made himself a large felt hat. Everyone laughed at it and made jokes about it. On his way back East he sold the hat for five dollars to a bull-whacker in St. Louis.

When he returned to Philadelphia he began manufacturing Stetson hats. His first product was called the "Boss of the Plains." He sent samples West and the hat became immediately popular. It was a natural-colored felt with a high crown and wide brim. There were many die-hards along the Rio Grande who would not wear one of these new-fangled hats. They insisted on the Mexican sombrero. These had a high crown and saucer-shaped brim with a plush surface often decorated with gold and silver

thread embroidery. The smart Mr. Stetson of Philadelphia made these, too, and they were sent to Mexico and imported into the United States. When John B. Stetson died in 1906 at the age of seventy-six, his firm had made thousands of hats and his name had passed into the language as a word for the cowboy hat. See HAT.

Sticky Looper. See RUSTLER.

Stirrup. A bent piece of wood or metal attached to the end of the saddle stirrup leather, which supports the rider's foot. Stirrups commonly are of tough wood, bent

into shape and bolted at the top, with the bottom part covered with rawhide. The cowboy rides with his foot jammed in the

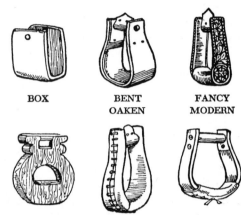

BOX   BENT OAKEN   FANCY MODERN

OLD CALIFORNIA   STEEL LEATHER   OX BOW
SOLID OAK   COVERED

stirrup to the heel of his boot, his toe pointing inward and either on a level with the ground or slightly downward. See SADDLE, TAPADEROS.

Stock Horse. A good working saddle horse on a ranch; one that works range stock. See HORSE.

Straw Boss. The assistant foreman on a ranch or second in charge on a cattle drive. Sometimes called *segundo* (say-goon'do), Spanish for "second." See CATTLE DRIVE.

String. Western term for a long, narrow strip of rawhide. It is also called "whang." Strings are cut from a disk or circular piece of rawhide, by spiraling around and around the outer edge. There is an art to cutting strings, as the natural skin or hide of an animal is thinner in some places, particularly that part which covers the belly. As the rawhide is cut while damp, experts cut the thinner portions wider and the thicker portions more narrow, so that when the string is stretched it is of consistent width.

Strings are used for many purposes, but mainly for braiding quirts, reins, headstalls, bosals, and reatas. Sometimes they are used for saddle strings after being softened with tallow or neat's foot oil. There are many stories of how rawhide strings shrink after drying. This is true only when they are green, that is, when cut off the fresh hide or skin. Such strings are used in lashing together posts and sideboards of a corral, repairing broken wagon tongues, and in the construction of simple furniture such as stools and chairs. The rafters and beams of the Mormon Temple at Salt Lake City were wrapped at the joints with green rawhide strings, instead of using nails, and ninety-five years later these rawhide bindings are still in use, hard as iron.

When rawhide strings have been stretched and dried they will not shrink after being dampened and allowed to dry again. The so-called "rawhide" shoe strings, yellow and grease-packed, which are sold commercially today, are not made of the rawhide the cowboy knows. See Bosal, Leather Braiding, Rawhide, Rope, Thong.

String-haltered. A horse that lifts his hind feet high up when in action is called "string-haltered."

Sudadero (soo-dah-day'roh). The leather lining of a saddle skirt. The word is Spanish and means "a handkerchief for wiping off the sweat." Hence it means a sweatband. See Saddle.

Sulker. In rodeo riding, the term for a horse that is hard to coax out of the chute and who squats back, bunches himself up, and then suddenly leaps forward. This is a hard horse to ride.

Surcingle. A girth or strap passing around the body of an animal.

Tail. To throw a young calf by swinging onto its tail. A full-grown steer or bull can be "tailed" by a man on horseback, but it

is a dangerous sport. The cowboy rides up alongside the animal, leans over and catches its tail in his right hand, gives it a couple of wraps around the saddle horn or once around his leg, and spurs his horse. The steer usually will make a complete somersault.

Tally. To count cattle. Cattle were counted at branding time, when they were being loaded for shipment, and often after a stampede on the trail. A man known as a

"tally man" might make such a record with pencil and paper. At other times a tally man filled his pockets with small stones, and as the cattle were driven before him in a line he would take a stone from the full pocket and put it in an empty one after each tenth cow. Or he might cut notches on a stick or tie knots in a string. See ROUNDUP.

Tapaderos (tah-pah-day'rohs). Usually called "taps." These are leather coverings

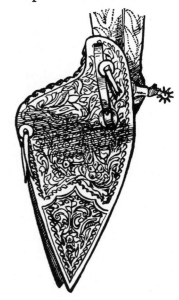

or shields over the front of the stirrups, used as a protection against brush and thorns. Some are carved and ornamented and are so long they almost touch the ground. Tapaderos are of Spanish origin. See SADDLE, STIRRUP.

Tarantula. A large, hairy spider of the West and Southwest. While they are poisonous, their bite is not necessarily fatal, and is treated much like a rattlesnake bite.

Many stories were told of these ugly creatures. It was said they could jump six feet or more. Cowboys would place two of them in a tub or large bowl and bet on which one would kill the other. A champion tarantula was highly prized and might be taken to fight another one on a ranch a hundred miles away. Cowboys learned one thing from such fights. A male tarantula would not attack a female or a relative. But females did not care—they would bite any other tarantula.

Tarp or **Tarpoleon.** Cowboy terms for tarpaulin, usually a canvas cover for a wagon or a packsaddle covering.

Tarrabee. A twisting paddle for spinning horsehair in making hair cinchas and hair ropes. "Tarrabee" was the cowboy's way of pronouncing *taravilla* (tar-ah-veel'-

lyah), the Mexican term. See CINCHA, HORSEHAIR ROPE.

Tenderfoot. This was a term the cowboy first gave to cattle imported from the East. Later he called men who came from the East by the same name. The plural of "tenderfoot" was "tenderfoots." A "regular" was the opposite of tenderfoot, meaning a seasoned Westerner. See PILGRIM.

Tepee. The wigwam or lodge of the Plains Indians. From fourteen to twenty-six poles were used in making a tepee, with one or two wing poles on the outside. The wing poles were for moving the wings near the opening at the top so the smoke could escape, and were always kept at the best angles for producing a draft. The covering of the tepee was made of buffalo hides, often decorated with crude drawings or designs. The tepee varied from sixteen to thirty feet in diameter at the floor. Many a cowboy slept overnight in the lodge or tepee of a friendly Indian tribe. See INDIAN.

Texas Rangers. The Texas Rangers were organized while Texas was still a part of Mexico. In their fights with western bad men, Indian marauders, Mexican cattle thieves, and others, they early gained a reputation for bravery and daring which became world wide.

149

In May, 1823, the Mexican governor of Texas, José Trespalacios, ordered the recruiting of a sergeant and fourteen men to protect colonists against the Indians. They were stationed near the mouth of the Colorado River. When the Indian trouble was over, Stephen F. Austin, the principal colonist, hired ten of the men at his own expense that same year. In 1826 these men helped whip a band of Indians who swooped down on the Colorado River settlements. After this the colonists agreed to keep a force of Rangers at all times.

As the colonists prepared to break away from Mexico, a council of Texans created a temporary corps to guard the border, and the same year, 1836, ordered a permanent battalion of 150 Texas Rangers established. These Rangers had to provide their own horses, saddles, and blankets. They received $1.25 a day as pay. They had no uniform, but dressed in buckskin coats, leather boots, and wide-brimmed felt hats. The Ranger's equipment and the way he lived was described thus in 1840: "Each man was armed with a rifle, a pistol, and a knife. With a Mexican saddle blanket tied behind his saddle and a small wallet in which he carried salt and ammunition and perhaps a little *panola,* or parched Indian corn, spiced and sweetened—a great allayer of thirst— and tobacco, he was equipped for a month. The little body of men, unencumbered by baggage wagons or pack trains, moved as lightly over the prairie as the Indians did, and as they did, traveled without tents. They slept with a saddle for a pillow at night, blankets over them, and their feet to the fire. Depending wholly upon wild game for food, they sometimes suffered the necessity of killing a horse for food. The men were splendid riders and used the Mexican saddle, improved somewhat by Americans, and carried the Mexican riata, made of rawhide, the cabrista, a hair rope, and the lariat to rope horses. Rangers frequently were divided into small parties and sent to different points for special purposes. When they started after Indians, even if the force was not large enough, they never came back until they caught them."[1]

The Rangers used the new Samuel Colt revolvers, and when Captain Samuel H. Walker of the Rangers suggested some improvements, Colt adopted them and called the new revolver the "Walker Colt," in honor of the Ranger captain. The Rangers gave it the name of "six-shooter."

The fighting ability of the Rangers was so respected that Sam Houston in 1858 shouted in the United States Senate: "Give me one thousand Rangers and we will be responsible for the defense of our frontier. Texas does not want regular troops. Withdraw them if you please." The deeds of the Rangers have been told in song and story. One old song went:

"Come listen to a ranger, you kind-
hearted stranger,
This song, though a sad one, you're
welcome to hear;
We've kept the Comanches away
from your ranches,
And followed them far o'er the Texas
frontier." [2]

The Rangers fought with the idea one of them expressed: " . . . no man in the wrong can stand up against a fellow that's in the right and keeps on a-comin'." In 1925 the Texas Rangers were abolished by a ruling of the lower courts, but a month later they were restored legally by the Supreme Court of Texas. In 1935 the force was modernized, and today the Rangers are a part of the Department of Public Safety of the State of Texas. They have a crime laboratory, bureaus of identification, and all modern

---

[1] From "Sketch of Col. James C. Hays, Texas Ranger," an old manuscript by John C. Caperton, quoted in an article in *The Western Horseman* by Wayne Gard.

[2] From John A. and Alan Lomax, *op. cit.*

equipment for detecting and catching law-breakers. They still wear no uniforms, as in the olden days, but they ride in fast automobiles instead of on Texas ponies. See BIBLE TWO, COLT, COMANCHE.

Texas Trail. See CATTLE TRAILS.

Texian. This was the old-time name for the Texan. During the days of the Republic of Texas they were called the "Fighting Texians." The people of Texas had to fight from the time Stephen F. Austin, the colonizer, went there to "redeem Texas from the wilderness." The Texians bought their liberty with blood. They held Texas together as a republic for nine years by fighting. The "Fighting Texians" made an everlasting name for themselves and were the ones who pushed back the frontiers and blazed the trails.

Thong. A long, narrow strip of leather. Thongs have replaced rawhide strings to a great extent in cowboy handicraft, and

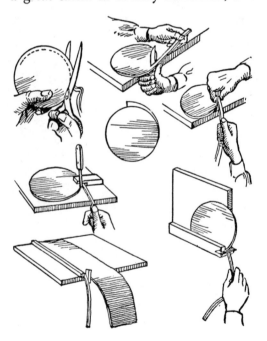

today quirts, headstalls, belts, and reins are usually braided from leather thongs rather than rawhide strings.

Thongwork has become a craft in itself. The leather thong does not have to be dampened when it is worked, it is more easily obtained, and can be bought in a variety of colors. Commercial thonging is cut as small as 3/32 of an inch in width and beveled so that it is flat when braided. The cowboy cuts his own thongs in much the same fashion as he does his rawhide strings, cutting them spiral fashion from a disk of leather. Shorter thongs are cut by placing the hide or skin on a hard surface and cutting the thong with a knife and straight-edge, or ruler. Thongs are used for fastenings and for holding pieces of leather together by edge braiding and by thong appliqué. Thongs are also woven into fancy buttons. See LEATHER, LEATHER BRAIDING, STRING.

Thoroughbred. A distinct breed of horse that is bred for speed alone. It was developed in England from Arabian stock, and trained for racing. The breed receives its name Thoroughbred because the horses are "thorough" or purebred. The word "Thoroughbred" is used loosely by people not connected with livestock to mean any purebred animal. "Purebred" is the proper word to use when one wants to show purity of ancestry as, a "purebred Morgan." But Thoroughbred is a distinct breed, and a "Thoroughbred Morgan" is one that is part Thoroughbred and part Morgan in ancestry. See HORSE.

Throw-back. Sometimes called "back-throw." The action of a horse when he rears and purposely throws himself back. As this is done usually by an outlaw or dangerous horse, the only way a rider can save himself, unless he can slip from the saddle, is to hit the horse a hard blow on the head with his loaded quirt in an effort to stun him. See OUTLAW.

Tie-Man. A cowboy who fastened the end of his rope tight to the horn of his saddle. See DALLY, HORN, ROPE, ROPING.

Tie Strings. Leather thongs which pass through leather or metal rosettes on the saddle. They help hold the saddle together, and the long ends are used to tie down ponchos, slickers, blankets, and other articles carried on his saddle by the cowboy. See CONCHA, ROSETTE, SADDLE.

Time. The old-time cowboy's term for his pay. He would say, "I'll draw my time."

Top Hand. A skillful and experienced cowboy. He draws the highest pay and generally rides the best saddle horses.

Top Off. A cowboy "tops off" a horse when he rides him. A term usually used in connection with riding a bucking horse.

Toppy Mounts. A term for good, reliable saddle horses.

Tortilla (tor-tee'yah). A very thin Mexican pancake made from ground maize, or corn meal. An important Mexican food item.

Tote. A good old word meaning to carry. A cowboy usually spoke of "toting" this or that. His favorite means of toting, however, was to lasso something and drag or "snake" it along at the end of his rope.

Town Marshal. The law enforcement officer of a town, a position similar to that of police chief. The town marshal was an important man in the wild cow towns of the West. He had to be a man without fear, a "quick-draw artist," and one who could shoot with deadly accuracy. Many times he was armed with two six-guns and a sawed-off shotgun, the latter loaded with buckshot. Men who had been former Texas Rangers were popular as town marshals.

Sometimes marshals were selected purposely for their reputation as killers and bad men, but in almost all instances when once on the side of the law they enforced it. Wild Bill Hickok already was known as a killer when he became marshal of Hays City, Kansas, and later of Abilene. Ben Thompson had a reputation as a bad man when he became marshal of Austin, Texas, and King Fisher of Uvalde County, Texas, had been at the head of a band of outlaws and had shown his contempt for the law by erecting a sign on a public thoroughfare which read: "This is King Fisher's Road. Take the Other." Wyatt Erp, marshal of Tombstone, and his brothers were notorious as bad men. William Barclay (Bat) Masterson, marshal of Dodge City, Kansas, was a killer, although it was said he "always killed philosophically."

The other type of marshal was the good citizen who always was on the side of justice and right. Notable among these were Patrick Floyd Garrett, of Lincoln County, New Mexico, who killed Billy the Kid;

Tom Smith, the marshal at Abilene, who used his fists instead of guns in subduing bad men; John Poe of the Panhandle; W. H. Middaugh of Denver, and Dallas Stroudenmire of El Paso, Texas. See BAD MAN, BONNEY, GUNFIGHTER, HICKOK.

Trace. The old-time word for trail. The cowboy spoke of a "cow trace."

Trail Boss. A man in charge of a herd being driven up the trail. The cowboy's saying was, "Keep one eye on the boss and two on the herd." See CATTLE DRIVE.

Travois (tra-voyce'). Two long poles attached to the sides of a horse, mule, or dog. The ends dragged on the ground and a basket was lashed between them. Indians used the travois to carry their baggage. Cowboys rigged up a travois when they had to carry a sick person to a town or hospital. See MEDICINE.

Tree. The frame of a saddle. It is built of hardwood and covered with rawhide. See SADDLE.

Trot. See GAIT.

Tumbleweed. The Russian thistle, a large weed of the western plains which, when dry, breaks off at the roots and is blown along by the wind. Some tumbleweeds are large as bushel baskets. Being round, they roll along easily. This is nature's way of scattering the plant's seeds.

Turkey. Wild turkeys were common in the West during the early days of the cowboy. While they were considered good

food by the cowboy, Indians would rarely eat turkey meat because they claimed it made them cowardly. The turkey is supposed to have received its name from its peculiar call of "turk, turk, turk."

Turtles. Members of the Cowboys Turtle Association, which is now the Rodeo Cowboys Association. Turtles wore a "Turtle Button," which indicated that they were professional rodeo contestants. See RODEO.

Two-Gun Man. A man wearing two six-guns, usually hung from a buscadero belt. The two-gun man was looked on with suspicion in the old days, and was considered either a show-off or a bad man, unless he was a town marshal or law officer. See BAD MAN, BELT, TOWN MARSHAL.

V-W-Y

Vamoose (va-moose'). The cowboy used this word several different ways. He would say to a companion, "Vamoose," and it would mean "Let's go," or "Let's hit the trail." He would shout at someone, "Vamoose!" and it would mean "Get out!" or "Get going!" He would say a man "vamoosed out of there," and this meant "he got out." The word came from the Spanish *vamos,* which means "we go."

Vaquero (vah-kay'roh). A Spanish word for cowboy, meaning the Mexican cowpuncher.

Vent Brand. A brand made by running a line through an old brand when a

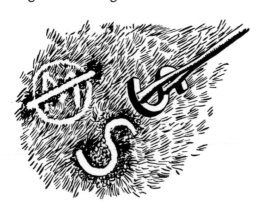

cow or horse was sold and placing on the new owner's brand. In other words, the old brand was cancelled. Also called a "counter brand." A cowboy spoke of "venting" a brand, and a "venting iron" was used to run a straight line through the former brand. The word is from the Spanish *venta,* meaning sale. See BRANDING IRONS, BRANDS.

Vest. The old-time cowboy usually wore a vest either of cloth or buckskin, not so much as an article of clothing as a place to carry small items. His vest pockets contained, among other things, matches and "the makin's," which were cigarette papers and a sack of Bull Durham. See HOLSTER VEST, "MAKINGS."

Vigilante. A member of a vigilance committee, or group of men organized in a section to protect their rights and deal with cattle thieves, outlaws, and murderers. Members of a vigilance committee would pass judgment on a man and hang him if they thought his crime was serious enough to deserve it.

The vigilance committee was a law unto itself. In many instances these committees were organized in districts where rustlers and bad men were not being punished by such courts of law as existed at the time, through influence or bribery. Sheriffs and town marshals in some counties and towns would not even arrest known criminals, either because they were secretly aligned with them or because they feared their vengeance. In the Denver Public Library today is preserved an original vigilante notice, which reads:

"VIGILANTES AROUND ! ! !
NO MORE MURDERS ! ! !
Behold the fate of this man. The same terrible end awaits all murderers. Life and the public security is too sacred not to be protected, even by a resort to the unpleasant means of *Lynch Law*.
TAKE WARNING! TAKE WARNING!
Else, ye murderers, the fate that this brute Schramie has met with awaits you.
By Order of Committee of *Vigilantes.*"[1]

This notice had been tacked to a tree from which the man named Schramie had been hanged by vigilantes. See LYNCHING.

Waddie. A slang name for cowboy. The term was first used in Wyoming in the late 1880's and the early 1890's, but in a slightly different sense. A "waddy" or "waddie" was a nester, small rancher, or freelance cowboy who rustled cattle from the big herds of wealthy cattlemen. This brought on the "Rustler War" in Wyoming in 1892. See RUSTLER, RUSTLER WAR.

Walk. See GAIT.

Walk Down. A method of catching

[1] From the original poster in The Denver Public Library.

wild horses or mustangs. The mustangers would follow a band of wild horses either on foot or horseback, or sometimes in a buckboard, keeping them on the move night and day until the horses became so tired they could be easily captured. There is one case recorded in which horse-catchers pursued a band of wild horses for nine days and nights, not allowing them to graze or take water, and finally captured forty-eight of them. See MUSTANG.

Walker Colt. See COLT, PISTOL, SIX-SHOOTER, TEXAS RANGERS.

Wallow-Stone. A round pebble, about the size of a pea, which a cowboy "wallows" around in his mouth when he is thirsty. It keeps the mouth and throat moist.

Wapiti (wop'i-tee). A large deer usually, and mistakenly, called elk by cowboys and other Westerners. They are common to the plains.

War Bag. A term for the early cowboy's traveling bag, generally an old gunny sack which had originally held grain or feed. In the Southwest he called it "war bag" or "war sack," but in the Northwest he might term it a "poke," meaning "parfleche," or "duffle bag." See DUFFLE BAG, PARFLECHE.

War Bridle. A halter used in leading unruly horses. It was nothing more than a lariat noose which was placed in a horse's

mouth and over his head. If the horse pulled against it, the noose tightened and cut his mouth.

Wash. Western term for a small stream.

Washtay. The Indian word for "good." "Heap washtay" meant "very good."

Water-Dog. A reptile half way between a lizard and a frog with smooth, shiny, naked skin. It is found near rivers and swamps. The only contact the cowboy had with these creatures was after a hard rain and in the vicinity of a marsh or river, when he might wake up in the morning and find one snuggled up in his blankets with him. They were sometimes known as hell-

benders, mud puppies, or water puppies.

Water-Hole Trap. The use of the water-hole trap was one of the best ways of catching wild horses. A circular corral was built around a water hole. A light-weight gate opened inward and was placed on the side from which the animals were in the habit of approaching. All other water holes in the vicinity were guarded by cowboys who frightened the horses away, so that they had to come to the one where the trap was built. Once they were inside, the gate was closed by a long rope, jerked by a cowboy hidden some distance away. See BLIND TRAP, CORRAL, MUSTANG.

Weanling. A foal, colt or filly, under one year old, that has been weaned from its mother. See COLT, FILLY.

Wear Leather. A protective covering on the honda, made of leather or rawhide. See HONDA, ROPE.

Wells Fargo. See OVERLAND STAGE.

Wells Fargo Colt. See COLT.

Westerner. People who lived on the eastern side of the Sierras and Cascades. People on the western side were called "Slopers."

Wet. The cowboy term for "stolen." It was first used along the Rio Grande when cattle were driven across the river. They were frequently sold while still wet.

Whale-Line. See ROPE.

Whipsaw. A cowboy term for getting the best of another fellow.

Whittling Pony. See CUTTING HORSE.

Wickey-up or **Wickiup.** A cowboy's temporary shelter for the night. It was usually a lean-to made by leaning several poles or tree limbs against a cross-bar or the side of a steep hill or rock and then covering the poles with a tarpaulin or blanket. More properly, a wickey-up was

a loosely constructed shelter used by Indians for a night's lodging when traveling. The cowboy also applied the term to the little house he used for his sweat bath. See MEDICINE.

Wildcatting. Acting recklessly or wildly. The term was commonly applied to the risks taken by a company of actors or entertainers who came into a cow town unbilled or without advance notice. The modern-day use of the term is in reckless or wild financing in oil wells.

Wild-Cow Milking. See RODEO.

Winchester. The cowboy term for a rifle or carbine. The first Winchester rifle was made by the Winchester Repeating Arms Company, of New Haven, Connecticut, in 1866. Oliver Winchester, a New England shirt manufacturer, had previously financed the New Haven Arms Company, which manufactured the Henry Repeating Rifle, a 15-shot rifle, in 1860. The 1866 Winchester was an outgrowth of the Henry rifle and used the same .44 caliber rim-fire

cartridge. But in 1873 Winchester put out his famous Model 73, which used a center-fire cartridge. This was the rifle which shared with the Frontier Model Colt revolver the major job of "winning the West." Extra-special Model 73 Winchesters were labeled "One in a Thousand" and sold for $100. These Winchesters were highly prized. The cowboy said the repeating Winchester could "shoot all week, including Sundays, without reloading."

Winchester made another popular rifle and carbine which appealed to the cowboy. This was the Model 1894, which used the new smokeless powder and took the equally famous 30-30 Winchester ammunition. Theodore Roosevelt carried one of these rifles on his African game hunt, and the 1,000,000th Winchester of the Model 94 was presented to President Calvin Coolidge. The famous Model 73 used by Buffalo Bill is still in existence. However, it is a smoothbore gun and used a miniature shotgun shell which enabled the great scout to break small glass balls in mid-air.

MODEL 73 WINCHESTER

Annie Oakley's Winchester, also a smoothbore, is on exhibition in the East. See BUFFALO BILL, CARTRIDGE, RIFLE.

Wind-broken. A term applied to a horse whose efforts to breathe are very noticeable.

Windmill. A machine by which the energy of the wind is applied to several useful purposes, such as grinding grain and pumping water. Windmills were used in Europe as far back as the twelfth century, mainly in Holland. The power comes from the action of the wind on "sails" which are arranged in the form of a wheel. It is estimated that the average windmill will work about eight hours out of twenty-four.

Windmills were not employed in the cattle country of the West and Southwest until barbed-wire fences were erected on the open range, thus keeping cattle from their natural watering places. At first cattlemen dug their own wells and pumped the water to the surface with "jack-pumps" or hand pumps. Persons called "switchers" located water by carrying a "water witch" or forked stick over the ground. They claimed that when water was underneath, the stick would "pull down." One of the first men to bring a windmill to the West was C. C. Slaughter, the cattle king of Spring County, Texas. In the 1870's windmills became popular and hardly a big ranch was without one. Ranches employed "windmill men" who were experts in caring for and repairing windmills. See BARBED WIRE, OPEN RANGE.

Winging. When a horse throws one foot out and is not true in his action, he is said to be "winging." See COLLECTED.

Wohaw. The Indian word for cow or beef. Indians would demand "wohaw" from trail bosses when the herds were being driven across their territory. The Indian coined the term from the "whoa" and "haw" of the ox drivers. See CATTLE DRIVE, INDIAN.

Wolf. As used by the cowboy, "wolf" generally meant the big gray timber wolf. These wolves would attack young cows and horses and hamstring them, then kill and eat them. Wolves did not begin to bother livestock until the buffalo began to grow scarce, as they formerly followed the buffalo herds. The timber wolf was known as the "lobo," from the Spanish word for wolf, the "loafer wolf," the "loper," and the "buffalo wolf."

These wolves sometimes traveled with two or more coyotes as companions and guides. The coyotes were more cunning than the wolves, and could lead them to their prey and warn them when danger was near. After the big wolf had killed an animal, the coyotes helped him eat it, in a strange partnership.

Some men made a specialty of killing wolves. They were known as "wolfers," and went from ranch to ranch, setting traps and laying poison. See COYOTE, HAMSTRINGING, WOLFER.

Wolfer. In the old days, a man who made a living killing wolves. He was an expert in setting traps and laying poison.

159

Wolfers were generally tough old fellows. Emerson Hough tells of one who carried his arsenic and tobacco in the same vest pocket, but the poison did not appear to bother him. See BURRO.

Wrangler. A cowboy who handles a string of extra saddle horses. The duty of the horse wrangler, sometimes called "remuda man," "nighthawk," or "cavvy man," is to guard the band of horses, see that they do not wander too far away, and produce them when the other cowboys want a change of horses. In the old days of the trail drives and roundups on the open plains, each cowboy usually had from five to nine extra mounts. He would ride one while the others were resting. The horse wrangler commonly is an ambitious young fellow who wants to be a full-fledged cowboy. He is the first man called in the morning by the cook and starts out to round up his band of horses and bring them to camp. In the cowboy's way of saying things, he "wrangles" his horses during the daytime and "herds" them at night. He "wrangles them" and does not "wrangle with them." See CATTLE DRIVE, REMUDA, ROUNDUP.

Wring-Tail. A term for a horse that nervously wrings or twitches his tail back and forth. This is usually done because the horse is in pain. "Wring-tails" are frequently seen in western movies and are supposed to be horses of spirit and action. But it will be noticed that they are being spurred or whipped and at the same time tightly reined in, and are in great pain.

Yearling. A male calf becomes a yearling on his first birthday. A female calf becomes a heifer. See CATTLE.

Yucca (yuk'a). A large plant with sharp-pointed, sword-like leaves and clusters of hanging, bell-like white flowers. It is common in the Southwest and Mexico. The plant sometimes grows as high as

twenty feet, and yuccas occur in such numbers as to form forests. The fibers of the leaves and stem are used by the Mexicans in making rope and string, and the fruit, which resembles a tiny banana, is cooked by Mexicans for food. The Mexican word is *yuca* (joo'kah).

BIBLIOGRAPHY

Books to read if you want to know more about—

Brands: *Hot Irons,* by Oren Arnold; *Cowboy Lore,* by Jules Verne Allen.

Buckaroos: *Californios,* by Joseph Jacinto Mora.

Cattle: *The Longhorns,* by J. Frank Dobie; *Cattle,* by William MacLeod Ráine and Will C. Barnes; *The Trampling Herd,* by Paul I. Wellman.

Cowboy Fiction: *The Virginian,* by Owen Wister; *North of 36,* by Emerson Hough; *Wolfville* and *Wolfville Days,* by Alfred Henry Lewis; *The Heart of the West,* by O. Henry.

Cowboy Songs and Ballads: *Cowboy Songs and Other Frontier Ballads,* by John A. Lomax and Alan Lomax.

Development of the West: *Roughing It,* by Mark Twain; *The Oregon Trail,* by Francis Parkman; *The Winning of the West,* by Theodore Roosevelt.

Dude Ranches: *Dude Ranches and Ponies,* by Lawrence Breese Smith.

Guns, Gunmen, and Gunfighters: *Triggernometry,* by Eugene Cunningham; *Famous Sheriffs and Western Outlaws* and *Guns of the Frontier,* by William MacLeod Raine; *The Story of the Outlaw,* by Emerson Hough.

History of the Cowboy: *The Cowboy,* by Philip Ashton Rollins; *The Cowboy and His Interpreters,* by E. Douglas Branch; *The Story of the Cowboy,* by Emerson Hough; *Trail Dust and Saddle Leather,* by Joseph Jacinto Mora.

History of the Horse in America: *The Horses of the Conquest,* by R. B. Cunninghame Graham; *The Horse of the Americas,* by Robert Moorehead Denhardt; *Justin Morgan Had a Horse,* by Marguerite Henry.

Illustrated Books by Western Authors: *Trails Plowed Under* and *Good Medicine,* by Charles M. Russell; *Pony Tracks* and *Crooked Trails,* by Frederic Remington.

Knots and Fancy Rope Work: *The Encyclopedia of Knots,* by Raoul Graumont and John Hensel.

Leather and Leather Braiding: *Leather Braiding,* by Bruce Grant.

Legends: *Pecos Bill,* by J. C. Bowman.

Modern Cowboys and Horses: *The Western Horseman* magazine and *The Horse Lover* magazine; *Cowboys and Cattle Kings,* by Charles Leland Sonnichsen.

Plains Indians: *The Fighting Cheyennes,* G. B. Grinnell; *Death in the Desert,* by Paul I. Wellman; *Sitting Bull,* by Stanley Vestal.

Pony Express and Stagecoaches: *The Pony Express,* by Arthur Chapman; *The Overland Mail,* by Le Roy Hafen.

Rodeos: *Hoofs and Horns* magazine; *El Rodeo,* by Charles Simpson; "Picked Up in the Rodeo Arena," by Jerry Armstrong, monthly feature in *The Western Horseman* magazine.

Rope Spinning and Roping: *Roping,* by Bernard S. Mason.

Texas: *Texas, A World in Itself,* by George Sessions Perry; *The Flavor of Texas,* by J. Frank Dobie; *The Raven,* by Marquis James.

Texas Rangers: *Captain Bill McDonald,* by Albert Bigelow Paine; *The Texas Rangers,* by Walter P. Webb.

True Stories of Early Cowboys: *The Log of a Cowboy,* by Andy Adams; *Riata and Spurs,* by Charles A. Siringo; *A Vaquero of the Brush Country,* by J. Frank Dobie.

PRINTED IN U.S.A.